S0-AKG-421

Professionalizing Business Analysis

Breaking the Cycle of Challenged Projects

Professionalizing Business Analysis

Breaking the Cycle of Challenged Projects

Kathleen B. Hass, PMP

ſſſ
MANAGEMENTCONCEPTS
8230 Leesburg Pike, Suite 800
Vienna, VA 22182
703.790.9595
Fax: 703.790.1371
www.managementconcepts.com

© 2008 by Management Concepts, Inc.

All rights reserved. No part of this book may be reproduced or utilized in any form or by any means, electronic or mechanical, including photocopying, recording, or by an information retrieval system, without permission in writing from the publisher, except for brief quotations in review articles.

Printed in the United States of America

Library of Congress Cataloging-in-Publication Data

Hass, Kathleen B.
  Professionalizing business analysis : breaking the cycle of challenged projects / Kathleen B. Hass.
    p. cm. -- (Business analysis essentials library ; Book 1)
  ISBN 978-1-56726-208-7
  1. Project management. 2. Strategic planning. 3. Business planning. 4. Organizational effectiveness. I. Title.

HD69.P75H376 2008
658.4'012--dc22   2007015069

10   9   8   7   6   5   4   3   2   1

About the Author

Kathleen B. Hass is the Project Management and Business Analysis Practice Leader for Management Concepts. Ms. Hass is a prominent presenter at industry conferences and an author and lecturer in the strategic project management and business analysis disciplines. Her expertise includes leading technology and software-intensive projects, building and leading strategic project teams, and conducting program management for large, complex engagements. Ms. Hass has more than 25 years of experience in project management and business analysis, including project portfolio management implementation, project office creation and management, business process reengineering, information technology (IT) applications development and technology deployment, project management and business analysis training and mentoring, and requirements management. Ms. Hass has managed large, complex projects in the airline, telecommunications, retail, and manufacturing industries and in the U.S. federal government.

Ms. Hass' consulting experience includes engagements with multiple agencies within the federal government, such as USDA, USGS, NARA, and an agency within the intelligence community, as well as industry engagements at Colorado Springs Utilities, Toyota Financial Services, Toyota Motor Sales, the Salt Lake Organizing Committee for the 2002 Olympic Winter Games, Hilti US Inc., The SABRE Group, Sulzer Medica, and Qwest Communications. Client services have included organizational maturity assessments, project quality and risk assessments, project launches, troubled project recovery, risk management, and implementation of program management offices and strategic planning and project portfolio management processes. Ms. Hass' professional experience includes work as an IT manager for Unisys Corporation and as Program Office Director for Albertson's Inc./American Stores Company.

Ms. Hass earned a B.A. in business administration with summa cum laude honors from Western Connecticut University.

To my husband, Jim, who has supported me throughout, with heartfelt gratitude.

Table of Contents

Part III – Other Considerations

Preface

The Business Analysis Essential Library is a series of books, each covering a separate and distinct area of business analysis. The business analyst is the project member who ensures that there is a strong business focus for business transformation projects that emerge as a result of the fierce, competitive nature and rapid rate of change of business today. Within both private industry and government agencies, the business analyst is becoming the central figure in leading major change initiatives. This library is designed to explain the emerging role of the business analyst and present contemporary business analysis practices (the what), supported by practical tools and techniques to enable the application of the practices (the how).

Current books in the series are:

+ *Professionalizing Business Analysis: Breaking the Cycle of Challenged Projects*

+ *The Business Analyst as Strategist: Translating Business Strategies into Valuable Solutions*

+ *Unearthing Business Requirements: Elicitation Tools and Techniques*

+ *Getting it Right: Business Requirement Analysis Tools and Techniques*

+ *The Art and Power of Facilitation: Running Powerful Meetings*

+ *From Analyst to Leader: Elevating the Role of the Business Analyst*

Check the Management Concepts website,
www.managementconcepts.com/pubs, for updates to this series.

Acknowledgments

I would like to thank Cleve Pillifant, Executive Director of the Project Management division at Management Concepts, for his leadership, passion, and vision. I would also like to offer my heartfelt appreciation to all of the contributing authors to the series: Kevin Brennan, Rosemary Hossenlopp, Lori Lindbergh, Richard Vander Horst, Don Wessels, Alice Zavala, and Kimi Ziemski.

I would also like to express my gratitude to Benjamin Nussbaum, editor of the series. Ben's gentle and very professional suggestions have greatly improved the flow and integration of the book series.

Part I
Introducing the Business Analyst

*T*he first section of this book lays the foundation for professionalizing business analysis. In Chapter 1, we discuss the nature of projects in organizations today, the reasons for the rather dismal project success rate, and the need for more rigorous business analysis to increase project success. We then define business analysis and explain how it is different from other analysis activities that occur in businesses today.

In Chapter 2, we explore the knowledge, skills, and abilities required to be a successful business analyst. We also discuss the collaborative relationship between the project manager and the business analyst, and finally, we discuss where the business analyst is placed in organizations.

In Chapter 3, we discover the importance of understanding project life cycles and provide an overview of the role of the business analyst throughout the business solution development life cycle.

Chapter 1

What Are Business Analysts and Why Are They Needed?

In This Chapter:

- The Problem with Projects
- Business Analysis Defined
- The Business Analyst and IT
- The History of Business Analysis

Change is the norm, fierce competition is the driver, and lean thinking is the latest call to action. Corporate survival depends on an ability to be nimble and to react appropriately and swiftly to change. It's even better to drive change, thus maintaining your competitive advantage in today's continually transforming marketplace. Organizations in both the public and private sectors are struggling not only to react to the high velocity of change in the economic, political, and global landscape but also to proactively stay ahead of the curve.

It is through projects that organizational leadership teams react to and plan for change. Projects play an essential role in the growth and survival of organizations today, for it is through projects that we create value in the form of improved business processes and new products and services. To manage change through projects, organizations need to professionalize business analysis knowledge, skills, and abilities so that they can (1) establish business strategies and goals,

(2) identify new business opportunities, (3) determine solutions to business problems, and (4) select, prioritize, and fund major change initiatives to meet business needs and achieve strategic goals.

The Problem with Projects

Projects today are large, complex, and high risk. Consider the characteristics of typical projects that are underway in virtually all public and private organizations of any size:

+ Business process improvement and/or reengineering ventures to replace inefficient and outmoded legacy business processes and technologies

+ Significant change programs to continually tune the organizational structure, capabilities, and competencies as the business model changes, including initiatives like organizational restructuring, outsourcing of core business processes, down- or right-sizing, staff acquisition and/or retooling, establishment or relocation of business operations, and mergers and acquisitions

+ New lines of business requiring design and implementation of new business processes, organizational structures, and technologies to support the new operations

These projects are further complicated by their significant technology component. Since data and information are the lifeblood of virtually all business processes, the information technology (IT) systems that provide the supporting technology to operate the business processes efficiently are often a major part of the business solution. As organizations engage in large change initiatives that depend more and more on technology for communications and operations, the business analysis contributions are becoming more and more essential in turning an organization's vision and strategy into reality.

A Track Record of Failure

It's worth looking at the track record for completion of complex projects that are accompanied by software-intensive IT systems. An abundance of surveys administered during the past decade reveal a rather dismal record of project performance, particularly for significant IT projects. The Standish Group's *2006 CHAOS Report* exposed the difficult nature of managing IT projects today: 46 percent of projects were challenged, meaning they were over time or budget, and an additional 19 percent of projects failed altogether, meaning nothing of value was delivered to the organization.[1]

**Figure 1-1—Results of the Standish Group's
2006 CHAOS Research Report**

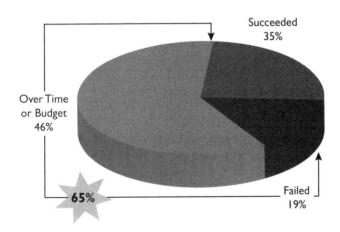

Source:
The Standish Group, 2006
CHAOS Report

Consult these authorities for the latest thinking in business analysis and project management best practices.

The Standish Group International, Inc., www.standishgroup.com, is a market research and advisory firm. The Standish Group provides critical information and active solutions to organizations concerned with developing and implementing business solutions. This advisory service is based on in-depth primary research supported by a rigorous process improvement cycle. Constant process improvement, coupled with a formal feedback system, ensures the latest in advanced thinking.

The Carnegie Mellon® Software Engineering Institute (SEI), www. sei.cmu, serves the nation as a federally funded research and development center. The SEI staff uses advanced software engineering principles and practices and has served as a national resource in software engineering, computer security, and process improvement. As part of Carnegie Mellon University, which is well-known for its highly rated programs in computer science and engineering, the SEI operates at the leading edge of technical innovation.

Studies by the Gartner Group and SEI also show the project management difficulties for software-intensive development endeavors. According to the Gartner and SEI research, 50 percent of software-intensive projects are rolled back out of production and 40 percent of problems are found by end-users. According to SEI, 25–40 percent of all spending on projects is wasted because of rework.

The Office of Management and Budget (OMB), the federal government agency that, among its other duties, evaluates the effectiveness of federal programs, policies, and procedures, has also compiled troubling statistics. A study published March 26, 2003, states that "…771 projects included in the fiscal 2004 budget—with a total cost of $20.9 billion—are currently at risk."[2]

The term *software crisis* is used to focus attention on the improvements needed for successful management of software-intensive projects.[3] Because the status quo cannot be tolerated, a number of government and industry initiatives have been spawned to address the problem:[4]

+ The Clinger-Cohen Act, passed by Congress in 1996 to instill private-sector IT management best practices in federal agencies. The law requires the largest agencies to create a CIO position to provide strategic insight into how IT can help mold the business processes used to deliver public services.

+ The U.S. Department of Defense's formation of the Software Engineering Institute at Carnegie Mellon University to promote mature, quality-based project management practices.

+ The formation of the Software Productivity Consortium, later renamed the Systems and Software Consortium, or SSCI (www.software.org), in the late 1980s to provide industry and government a resource for insight, advice, and tools that could help address the complex and dynamic world of software and systems development.

+ The development of sophisticated educational programs like the Defense Systems Management College on the Management of Software Acquisition and the graduate software engineering program at George Mason University.

+ The development of advanced standards, such as DoD acquisition standards 2167 and 2168.

+ The DoD Software Technology for Adaptable, Reliable Systems (STARS) program, which established the foundation for the integrated tool environment.

+ The formation of the IT Governance Institute, or ITGI (www.itgi.org), in 1998 to advance international thinking and standards in directing and controlling IT groups to ensure that IT supports business goals, optimizes business investment in IT, and appropriately manages IT-related risks and opportunities. Also from ITGI, the Control Objectives for Information and Related Technology (COBIT) provides a comprehensive framework for the management and delivery of high-quality IT-based services.

* The formation and success of the Project Management Institute, long acknowledged as a pioneer in the field of project management. The Institute has a truly global membership of more than 200,000 professionals, representing 125 countries.

* And most recently, the emergence of the International Institute of Business Analysis (IIBA), founded in 2003, an organization dedicated to advancing the professionalism of the business analysis occupation. The IIBA is the independent nonprofit professional association that serves the growing field of business analysis. Its membership consists of persons with various titles, filling a diverse set of roles—requirements engineers, systems analysts, business analysts, requirements analysts, project managers, technical architects and developers, consultants, and, in fact, anyone involved in analysis for systems, business, or process improvement.

A Solution: Better Requirements Engineering

There is a growing notion that poor requirements engineering is one of the leading causes of project failure. Requirements are hard—very hard—to get right, especially for software. It is becoming clear that business solution development must be treated as a specialist discipline, implementing requirements formed through good requirements capturing, documenting, and managing techniques. Consider these observations, which were retrieved from www.theiiba.org and come from experts in the field:

> Communication challenges between business teams and technologists are chronic—we estimate that 60%–80% of project failures can be attributed directly to poor requirements gathering, analysis, and management.
>
> *Meta Group Research (now Gartner)*

> Poorly defined applications have led to a persistent miscommunication between business and IT that largely contributes to a 66% project failure rate for these applications, costing U.S. businesses at least $30B every year.
>
> *Forrester Research*

> 56% of defects can be attributed to requirements, and 82% of the effort to fix defects.
>
> *James Martin*

The obvious conclusion: existing requirements engineering approaches, methods, and tools simply don't deliver the results that are vital for the success of organizations, both public and private. Because businesses across the globe rely on successful business transformation projects with critical IT components for their very survival, the stakes are too high to continue in business-as-usual mode.

The requirements engineering process—when conducted using best practices—is typically composed of activities like scope or context definition, requirements elicitation, requirements analysis, requirements specification, requirements documentation, requirements validation and verification, and requirements management. These subdisciplines encompass the activities involved in gathering, evaluating, documenting, and managing changes to requirements.

It is widely believed that the use of effective requirements definition and management practices leads to successful projects, satisfied customers, and increased professionalism in the industry. The elements that must be in place to produce high-quality requirements include:

+ A representative group of key stakeholders who understand the needs of the business

+ A project champion who plays an active role in requirements definition

+ A strong commitment to project objectives on the part of the project team

+ Use of a repeatable requirements engineering process, tools and techniques that are continually improved

+ An understanding of the business architecture that supports the current and planned needs of the business, accompanied by an aligned technology architecture

+ The ability to accommodate changes in requirements as those requirements are progressively elaborated

In a response to the belief that more rigorous attention to requirements management will add considerable value to project team effectiveness and greatly improve project performance, business analysis is emerging as a valued business competency.

Business Analysis Defined

There's no standard definition of *business analysis* in organizations today. Some organizations restrict business analysis to the process of requirements elicitation, analysis, and change management. These processes encompass gathering requirements from the customer; structuring requirements by classes or categories; evaluating requirements for selected qualities; modeling requirements to further represent their relationships; decomposing requirements into more detail; finalizing requirements in the form of documents, diagrams, matrices, and tables; and then managing subsequent changes to the requirements.

Other organizations broaden the definition to include financial analysis, quality assurance, organizational development, testing and training, and documentation of business policies and procedures. Indeed, in many organizations a person might play multiple project team roles concurrently while being dubbed the project manager or systems manager. The same person might be the project manager, technical lead, and business analyst.

Business analysis is emerging as a professional field, and so standard definitions and role delineation are emerging as well. The IIBA definition of business analysis is the definition we will use in the Business Analysis Essential Library series:[5]

> Business analysis is the set of tasks, knowledge, and techniques required to identify business needs and determine solutions to business problems. Solutions often include a systems development component, but may also consist of process improvement or organizational change.

In this definition, the role of the business analyst differs considerably from the traditional role of the IT systems analyst in that the business analyst is focused exclusively on the business need and adding business value.

The Business Analyst and IT

Business analysts get involved and play a leadership role in many nontechnical projects. Examples include development of the business architecture, business process reengineering, competitive analysis and benchmark studies, pre-project analysis, business case development, and organizational restructuring and relocating. In practice, business analysis is an essential component of project success, regardless of whether technology is involved.

However, the IT systems that provide the supporting technology to operate the business processes efficiently are often a major component of large projects. Indeed, superior IT systems are now becoming a competitive advantage to organizations. Although there are business-related projects that do not involve IT, these projects are becoming increasingly rare. Today's business analysts recognize they must be fluent in both the business and technology domains.

In analyzing the root cause of the current state of failed and challenged business projects, we have learned that the talents, competencies, and heroics of project managers, business visionaries, and technologists alone cannot drive value into the organization. For business needs and goals to be converted into innovative solutions that truly bring wealth to the enterprise, a stronger bridge must be built between the business community and the technical community. That bridge is built by employing the practices of professional business analysis prior to and during the development of the business transformation solutions.

IT managers are realizing that technical skills can be relatively easy to outsource, but that they cannot abdicate control of their business requirements. In virtually every organization, the elevated leadership role of the business analyst is beginning to shape the future of business transformation.

It is increasingly clear that although technical knowledge areas are necessary, they are insufficient for successfully managing requirements on the large, enterprise-wide, complex, mission-critical projects that are the norm today. Just as business leaders must be multi-skilled and strategically focused, business analysts must possess an extensive array of leadership skills. The business analyst is now assuming a leadership role and is quickly rising to a senior position in the enterprise. As the IT contribution moves beyond efficiency to business effectiveness, the business analyst becomes the central figure on the project team who is bilingual—speaking both business and technical languages. To perform in this pivotal role, the business analyst must have a broad range of knowledge, skills, and competencies. Without this key liaison between the business and IT departments, poor requirements definition emerges, resulting in a disconnect between what IT builds and what the business needs.

The History of Business Analysis

Business analysis is just now emerging as a recognized occupation. That is not to say that no one in the business world conducted analysis in the past. On the contrary, several analyst roles are commonly found in organizations, including financial analyst, quality assurance analyst, and IT systems analyst. However, it is just now becoming clear that a business analyst is needed as a critical member of a project team if organizations intend to use projects to sustain or secure their competitive advantage.

In many organizations, the role of the business analyst and the competencies necessary to perform that role have not been differentiated from those of other analysts residing in the business, from those of systems analysts residing in the technical group, or from those of a subject matter expert or a project manager. Yet, all of these roles have very distinct responsibilities during the life of the project. It is no wonder projects fail at a high rate when project team members are expected to perform skillfully even when their required competencies have not been clearly defined. In fact, even the titles of the individuals performing business analysis activities on projects still vary widely—systems analyst, solutions architect, systems engineer, requirements engineer, and even project manager are all titles given to individuals who perform business analysis.

Recognizing the need for rigorous business analysis on projects and the need to put order to this relative chaos, the IIBA was founded in 2003 to advance the professionalism of the business analysis occupation. The IIBA is developing the *Business Analysis Body of Knowledge* (*BABOK*™) for the profession. In this quest, the IIBA works with "practitioners around the globe to continually add to those standards through education, research, and the sharing of effective tools and techniques."[6] In addition, the IIBA has developed a Business Analyst Certification Program unique to the profession of business analysis. Establishing a certification for business analysis will go a long way in standardizing and professionalizing the practice of business analysis. The certification creates a standard vernacular and standardizes organizations' expectations for the knowledge, skills, and competencies of a Certified Business Analyst.

Endnotes

1. The Standish Group International, Inc. *Unfinished Voyages: A Follow-Up to The Chaos Report*, 1999. Online at www.standishgroup.com/sample_research/unfinished_voyages_1.php (accessed April 8, 2005).

2. Federal IT Project Manager Initiative. Online at www.ocio.usda.gov/p_mgnt/doc/CIO_Council_Guidance.ppt#425,1, Federal IT Project Manager Initiative (accessed December 27, 2005).

3. U.S. General Accounting Office. *Defense Acquisitions: Stronger Management Practices Are Needed to Improve DOD's Software-Intensive Weapon Acquisitions*, Report to the Committee on Armed Services, March 2004. Online at www.gao.gov/new.items/d04393.pdf (accessed January 2007).

4. Kenneth E. Nidiffer and Dana Dolan. "Evolving Distributed Project Management," *IEEE Software*, September/October 2005. Online at www.computer.org/software (accessed January 2007).

5. International Institute of Business Analysis. *Business Analysis Body of Knowledge*, draft version 1.6, 2007. Online at www.theiiba.org/pdf/BABok_Release_1dot4_2005Oct27.pdf (accessed December 21, 2006).

6. International Institute of Business Analysis. Online at www.theiiba.org (accessed December 21, 2006).

Chapter 2

The Business Analyst in the Organization

In This Chapter:

- Will the Real Business Analyst Please Stand Up?
- The Business Analyst and the Project Manager
- Where Will the Business Analyst Reside?

Will the Real Business Analyst Please Stand Up?

Expectations for the business analyst are high and growing. Browsing through the more than 5,000 job postings for business analysts on Monster.com turned up this lofty job description:

> The main purpose of the role will be to design and specify innovative solutions which meet the business requirements allowing the business benefit to be attained; and to facilitate divisional communication and awareness of the standards and quality expectations within the System Analyst teams.

Many job titles were also uncovered, including business analyst, business systems analyst, business system planner, and even principal solutions architect. Regardless of the job title, a strong, experienced business analyst is critical to project success. Simply put, without well-understood and well-documented requirements, it is virtually impossible to meet project objectives. If an organization has only the resources and budget to invest in a single life cycle area to improve project performance, that area should be requirements definition and management.

Depending on the business analyst's level of responsibility and placement in the organization, the analyst's duties include the following:

+ Identify and understand the business problem and the impact of the proposed solution on the organization's operations

+ Document the complex areas of project scope, objectives, and the added value or benefit expectations using an integrated set of analysis and modeling techniques.

+ Translate business objectives into requirements using powerful analysis and modeling tools

+ Evaluate customers' business needs, thus contributing to strategic planning of information systems and technology directions

+ Assist in determining the strategic direction of the organization

+ Liaise with major customers during preliminary installation and testing of new products and services

According to a 2006 custom research study conducted by Evans Data Corporation for COMPUWARE and the Requirements Networking Group, the typical business analyst is 40 years old, well-educated, and paid at least $78K per year.[1] Most hail from IT and have more than five years of experience performing analyst functions. Most of the analyst skills have been acquired along the way, as the individual's interest has migrated from the technology to the business. And, disturbingly, the respondents reported that most of their projects do not deliver all requirements.

The study goes on to conclude that business analysts are still assigned activities that are different from business analysis, including project management, programming, design, and functional management. While the majority of time spent by business analysts is used documenting and managing requirements, business analysts tend to be involved in a wide range of activities, including project management, solution development, testing, and serving as experts in certain domains.

Various Roles Performed by the Business Analyst	Percentage of Time
Business Analyst	29.3
Project Management	18.7
Developer, Engineer, Development Lead	15.4
Subject Matter Expert, Domain Expert	13.5
Tester, Test Lead	10.1
Other	13.0
Total	100.0

To support important change initiatives, a technically adept engineer is sometimes asked to serve as business analyst along with performing his or her technical role. Sometimes a person assumes a trio of leadership roles on a project—technical lead, project manager, and business analyst. Once requirements are captured at a high level and the project plan is being executed, technical activities tend to demand most of this person's attention. When that happens, requirements and project management suffer, and the initiative is positioned to become a runaway project. Make no mistake: using the same person as a technical lead, project manager, and business analyst has contributed significantly to challenged and failed projects.

As a result of the ambiguity that exists both in role definition and competency requirements, organizations are attempting to define a career path for business analysts. See Table 2-1 for our recommended business analyst career path.

Table 2-1—Business Analyst Career Path

Level	Proficiency	Responsibilities
Strategic	Ability to perform strategic tasks with minimal direction	**Strategic Planning** • Provide competitive information to the executive team • Facilitate strategy sessions • Draft and maintain strategic plans, goals, and measures **Enterprise Analysis** • Develop and maintain the business architecture; define business problems and opportunities • Conduct feasibility studies to analyze potential solutions; identify optimal solution • Develop the business case for proposed new projects • Develop tools, processes, and policies for portfolio management • Facilitate portfolio management sessions • Measure the value of new business solutions and compare to benefit estimate in business case • Conduct root-cause analysis if the benefit was not obtained **Mentor Senior-Level BAs**
Senior	Ability to perform complex tasks with minimal coaching	*For Significant High-Risk Projects* **Elicit Requirements** • Conduct elicitation sessions: interviews, surveys, focus groups, workshops **Analyze and Specify Requirements** • Construct complex models—process, data, workflow, object-oriented, use-cases, functional decomposition diagrams, etc. • Develop business architecture: as-is/to-be models • Analyze and manage requirement risk • Structure requirements for traceability • Prioritize requirements • Draft requirement specifications **Document, Validate, and Manage Requirements** • Finalize the requirements artifact set • Plan and conduct structured quality reviews of requirements and solutions • Develop test plans • Support technical team • Manage User Acceptance Test activities • Manage changes to requirements **Solution Delivery, O&M** • Manage customer acceptance of new business solutions • Analyze help desk requests • Conduct root-cause analysis of problems • Plan and implement continuous improvement of the solution • Administer customer satisfaction surveys • Measure the value of new business solutions and compare to benefit estimate in business case • Conduct root-cause analysis if the benefit was not obtained **Mentor Intermediate-Level BAs**

Level	Proficiency	Responsibilities
Interme-diate	Ability to perform simple to moderately complex tasks with minimal assistance	**For Small to Moderate-Risk Projects** **Elicit Requirements** • Conduct elicitation sessions: interviews, surveys, focus groups, workshops **Analyze and Specify Requirements** • Construct models—process, data, workflow, object-oriented, use-cases, functional decomposition diagrams, etc. • Develop business architecture: as-is/to-be models • Analyze and manage requirement risk • Structure requirements for traceability • Prioritize requirements • Draft requirement specifications **Document, Validate, and Manage Requirements** • Finalize the requirements artifact set • Plan and conduct structured quality reviews of requirements and solutions • Develop test plans • Support technical team • Manage User Acceptance Test activities • Manage changes to requirements **Solution Delivery, O&M** • Manage customer acceptance of new business solutions • Analyze help desk requests • Conduct root-cause analysis of problems • Plan and implement continuous improvement of the solution • Administer customer satisfaction surveys • Measure the value of new business solutions and compare to benefit estimate in business case • Conduct root-cause analysis if the benefit was not obtained **Mentor Junior-Level BAs**
Associate	Ability to perform simple tasks with assistance	**Support Intermediate and Senior BAs** • Review and compile results of interviews and surveys • Scribe interview notes and workshop output • Build simple models • Provide support for the help desk

Staffing surveys reveal an increasing demand for senior-level individuals who can perform the ever-widening range of business analysis functions. Because business analysts walk in both the business and IT worlds, they arrive from various fields. We have learned that most come from the ranks of programmer and analyst positions, whereas others have conventional business expertise supplemented by some IT training. To successfully fill the business analyst role, one must acquire mastery of a unique combination of technical, analytical, business, and leadership skills. See Table 2-2, Business Analyst Knowledge and Skill Set Requirements.

Table 2-2—Business Analyst Knowledge and Skill Set Requirements

Technical	Analytical	Business	Leadership
Systems engineering concepts and principles	Fundamentals of business analysis	Business process improvements and reengineering	Fundamentals of project management
Complex modeling techniques	Ability to conceptualize and think creatively	Strategic and business planning	Capacity to articulate vision
Communication of technical concepts to nontechnical audiences	Techniques to plan, document, analyze, trace, and manage requirements	Communication of business concepts to technical audiences	Organizational change management; management of power and politics
Testing, verification, and validation	Requirements risk assessment and management	Business outcome thinking	Problem solving, negotiation, and decision-making
Technical writing	Administrative, analytical, and reporting skills	Business writing	Team management, leadership, mentoring, and facilitation
Rapid prototyping	Cost/benefit analysis	Business case development	Authenticity, ethics, and integrity
Technical domain knowledge	Time management and personal organization	Business domain knowledge	Customer relationship management

The Business Analyst and the Project Manager

At the center of the core project team is the dynamic twosome—the project manager and the business analyst. The project manager focuses on the management of the project, while the business analyst focuses on the management of the business requirements and business value. The wise project manager welcomes the business analyst, understanding that inadequate information relating to requirements leads to poor estimates and makes time and cost management virtually impossible. Project managers rely on business analysts to assist in providing:

+ More detailed project objectives

+ Business needs analysis

+ Clear, structured, usable requirements

+ Trade-off analysis

+ Requirement feasibility and risk analysis

+ Cost/benefit analysis

Obviously, these activities differ from the traditional systems analyst's focus, which often leaps over business requirements and focuses on writing system specifications.

Combining disciplines leads to success. To increase the rate of project success, executives are adopting the discipline of project management and superior business analysis as strategic business practices. Instead of the project manager being the final arbiter, the new way of doing things is more about leadership and collaboration. Project managers and business analysts are collaborating with core technical and business team members throughout the project to increase the probability of project success.

As collaboration increases, it is important to clearly identify roles and responsibilities. The responsibility assignment matrix (RAM) is a structure that links resources to tasks to help ensure that each element of the project's scope of work is assigned to a responsible in-

Collaboration Opportunities Between the Business Analyst and the Project Manager

- Creation of:
  - Business case
  - Charter
  - High-level scope statement
  - Preliminary (high-level) plan
  - Risk assessment
- Establishing project priorities
- Stakeholder identification and management
- Getting the right people involved and excited about the potential project
- Partnering with senior IT architecture team to create product's "vision"
- Requirements elicitation workshops
- Iterations (agile, etc.) life cycle choice
- Rolling-wave plan development
- Early solution alternative analysis
- Trade-off analysis for the requirements and solution trade-offs
- Balancing the competing demands of scope, cost, time, quality, and risk
- Requirements validation
- Control gate sign-off and go/no go decisions
- Test plan and test approach
- Early validation activities
- Test results review
- Defect root-cause analysis and corrective action
- Issue management
- Go/no go decision to deliver:
  - Deployment plan
  - Approach
  - Which business units are affected?
  - When will the business units be implemented?
  - When will training be delivered?
  - When will post-implementation support by the core project team end?
- Decision to close the project and move to operations and maintenance
- Lessons learned
- Prioritization of enhancements
- Root-cause analysis of performance and value attainment issues after delivery

dividual. It lists individuals and their responsibility type (see Figure 2-1). The legend for the responsibility types is:

+ **Responsible (R)**—The individual(s) who actually completes the work.

+ **Accountable (A)**—The individual who is ultimately accountable that the work is completed with quality. Only one "A" can be assigned to a deliverable.

+ **Consulted (C)**—The individual(s) to be consulted prior to a final decision.

+ **Informed (I)**—The individual(s) to be informed after a decision or action is taken.

+ **Sign-Off Required (S)**—The individual(s) to provide final approval sign-off for a deliverable.

Figure 2-1—Sample RAM

Deliverable	Project Manager	Business Analyst	Business Lead	Technical Lead
A	A	I	S	R
B	C	R/A	S	I
C	I	C	S	R/A

Where Will the Business Analyst Reside?

As organizations struggle to implement contemporary business analysis practices, they are wrestling with tough decisions regarding how to design the optimum structure for incorporating the business analyst into the organization. Does it make sense to have business analysts centralized, reporting to a neutral organization like Finance, IT, or an enterprise project management office (PMO)? Or should business analysts report to individual business units? Should business analysts and project managers report to the same functional manager?

Although there is no one right answer to the organizational placement of business analysts, there are some general guidelines. For mid-level business analysts (those who manage day-to-day operational issues and also coordinate the IT application system maintenance and enhancement projects), both the decentralized model, where the business analysts are placed in the business units, and the centralized model, where they reside in IT, are used. Both models have challenges that must be understood and managed.

+ When mid-level business analysts are placed in IT, an unintended consequence might emerge: the business might not take ownership of its technology needs, and the business analyst might begin to speak for the business, as opposed to bringing the business into the decision-making process. In this case, IT management needs to reach out to the business units to conduct working sessions and ensure that the appropriate business SMEs are fully engaged in decisions regarding IT support, maintenance, and enhancement work.

+ When mid-level business analysts are decentralized in one group and placed in the various business units, it is difficult for them to feel like a "community of practice" and hard for the organization to manage consistency, standards, improvement of the business analysis process, and advancement of the business analysis profession within the organization. In addition, these business analysts tend to be more removed from IT and might not possess an adequate understanding of the IT domain. In this instance, IT should foster communities of practice through which the business analysts can get together as a team for mentoring, training, lessons learned, improvement of methods and tools, etc.

It is important for senior-level business analysts to be part of an enterprise-wide PMO or center of excellence (CoE) with a strategic focus. This is because strategic projects are usually cross-functional and are often enterprise-wide. Placement in some sort of an enterprise-wide office allows senior business analysts to:

+ Provide pre-project support in identifying new business opportunities, conducting feasibility studies, conducting alternative analysis for the most optimum solution, and then developing the business case for new projects to be submitted to management for project selection and prioritization.

+ Serve as the business analyst (or the lead of a business analyst team, for a large program with supporting projects) for strategic, high-risk, complex projects. This allows the business analyst to ensure that requirements are fully understood and to continually validate that the solution will meet the business need during the entire solution development life cycle.

+ Continually validate that the business case remains viable and the project investment is sound.

In addition, discussions are taking place across IT organizations about the role of business analysts. Should business analysts be line managers? Should they be fully dedicated to requirements? Should they have "other responsibilities as assigned?" Do organizations typically have multiple business analyst levels?

Business analysts are not typically line managers. However, a pool of business analysts might report to a manager who is a senior business analyst. For high-risk, complex projects, a senior business analyst should be dedicated full-time to the project with no other responsibilities (as should be a senior project manager). Organizations are learning that business analysis is a profession, and that the business analyst needs to master business analysis knowledge, skills, and practices to become a strategic asset to the enterprise. As a result, "other duties as assigned" is not recommended. Organizations typically have several levels of business analysts; for small, low-risk projects, a business analyst likely works on more than one project concurrently.

Endnote

1. Evans Data Corporation. "The New Business Analyst: A Strategic Role in the Enterprise," 2006. Online at www.compuware.com/thenew strategicBA (accessed January 2007).

Chapter 3

Business Analysis through Life Cycles

In This Chapter:

- Understanding Project Life Cycles

- The Business Solution Life Cycle

- The Systems Requirements Life Cycle

For an in-depth discussion of business analysis practices, it is helpful to frame the dialogue in the context of a generic project life cycle. Refer to Figure 3-1, the Business Solution Life Cycle, to provide context as we examine the requirements engineering subdisciplines. The figure shows a sequential development approach, from strategic planning and project selection to managing business requirements to the delivery of a complete operational capability. It is a simplistic model that shows the system engineering process through its typical phases.

Figure 3-1—Business Solution Life Cycle

Deliverables

Skills and Techniques

Business Value Attainment

Operations Period

Implementation Period

Study

Business Solution Life Cycle

Systems Requirements Life Cycle

Deliverables	Business Solution Life Cycle	Systems Requirements Life Cycle	Skills and Techniques
System Maintenance and Enhancements	Deactivate / Operations & Maintenance	Operations & Maintenance	Change Management Tools
System Delivery Post-Implementation Support	Deliver	Deliver	User Surveys and Interviews
Functional Tests Supplemental Tests User Acceptance Test	Test	Test	Verification Techniques Validation Techniques
Development Code-Based Tests	Construction	Trace	
		Manage Change	
Requirements Change Management Plan Requirements Traceability Matrix Outsource Test Decision Request for Proposal (RFP) Test Plan Test Cases Test Scenarios	Design	Prototype	Change Management Tools Requirements Allocation Techniques
		Trade-Off Analysis	
		Mitigate Risks	Risk Monitoring and Control Tools
		Allocate and Trace	Prototyping Techniques
User Class Analysis Requirements Management Plan Feature Prioritization Matrix Requirements Documentation Requirements Feasibility Alternatives Study Requirements Baseline Outsource Development Decision Request for Proposal (RFP)	Requirements	Documentation and Validation	Requirements Gathering Tools Requirements Facilitation Skills Requirement Writing Skills Early Requirement Verification Techniques Partitioning and Decomposition of Requirements Risk Planning Techniques Risk Identification Techniques Risk Analysis and Response Planning Tools Prototyping Techniques Feasibility and Alternatives Analysis Techniques
		Specification	
		Analysis	
		Elicitation	
Business Case High-Level Product Description Project Charter Statement of Work	Enterprise Analysis	Business Domain Scope Definition	Value Management Techniques Facilitation and Consensus Building Skills Conflict Management Skills Decision-Making Techniques Key Performance Indicator Development Stakeholder Management Skills Requirements Presentation Skills
		Business Need	
Strategic Plan Strategic Goals	Strategic Planning		

The figure shows a business solution life cycle, which is being used to illustrate a generic project life cycle, and a corresponding systems requirement life cycle. The systems requirement life cycle is a subset of the larger business solution life cycle. Throughout the entire business solution life cycle, the business analyst serves as the liaison between the business community and the technical solution providers. However, most business analysts do most of their work within the systems requirements life cycle.

Before we discuss the business analyst's role in detail, let's explore the importance of life cycles. This chapter delves into both the business solution life cycle and the systems requirements life cycle. The chapters in Part II discuss the role of the business analyst in the context of the phases of the business solution life cycle and the subphases of the system requirements life cycle.

Understanding Project Life Cycles

Before we put requirements in the context of a project's typical life cycle phases and activities, a few definitions are needed.[1] A *project life cycle* is a collection of sequential project stages, whose names and number are determined by the control needs of the organization involved in the project. A project life cycle represents the highest-level project management approach, depicted as a series of periods and phases, each with a defined output. A project life cycle can be documented with a *methodology*, which is a system of practices, techniques, procedures, and rules used by those who work in a discipline. A project methodology is a documented set of steps and rules that apply to each stage and are designed to provide repeatable performance in accomplishing a project.

A *period* is the highest-level division of the project life cycle, as in the study, implementation, and operations periods depicted in Figure 3-1. Project periods are decomposed into *phases, subphases, activities, products,* and *control gates*. Within each period are multiple phases.

For example, the phases within the implementation period are requirements, design, construction, test, and deliver.

- *Phases* and *subphases* are composed of a collection of logically related project activities, usually culminating in the completion of a major deliverable and marked by a project *milestone*. A *milestone* is a significant, measurable project event usually marked by a management review and decision to proceed, often referred to as a *control gate review*.

- *Activities* are operations or tasks that consume time and resources to produce the products of the project. An activity is the smallest unit of work within a project network and work breakdown structure.

Although the steps in project life cycles appear to be sequential, they are unquestionably performed iteratively. Iterating is an effective strategy when attempting to control an unpredictable process like business process design and IT solution development. Customer feedback mechanisms are planned at frequent intervals during the project life cycle to uncover defects and apply corrections as early in the project as possible, when the cost of correction is lower.

The key to acquiring feedback early and often is an iterative approach to requirements generation. During the requirements phase, when the business analyst is determining the business requirements, the IT architects are working on early iterations of the solution design. As the business analyst conducts requirements trade-off analyses, the architect does the same on solution options.

The Business Solution Life Cycle

The business solution life cycle presented in Figure 3-1 is a standard project life cycle depicting the typical phases involved in developing a new business system. Sometimes the term *business system* is used to refer only to the IT system, but make no mistake—a complete business system is composed of the elements listed below. To avoid confusion, we are using the terms *business solution* and *business system* synonymously and in the broad sense, in which they include:

+ Business policies, processes, and procedures

+ Organizational entities that own and operate the business system

+ Geographic locations of the organizational entities

+ Data that flow through the business processes and IT systems

+ IT application systems that support the operation of the business system

+ Technology infrastructure supporting the applications

The development of a new or reengineered business application system might involve changes to some or all of the business system components. The periods and phases depicting the business solution development life cycle include the following. A brief explanation of the business analyst's role in each phase is provided.

+ **Study period**

  □ **Strategic planning phase.** Develop organizational vision, mission, strategies, and goals. The business analyst may provide information or facilitate strategy sessions.

  □ **Enterprise analysis phase.** The business analyst facilitates and collaborates in identifying business opportunities to achieve the goals, exploring potential solutions, identifying the optimal solution, and preparing the business case to propose a new project.

+ **Implementation period**

  □ **Requirements phase.** The business analyst facilitates and collaborates in eliciting, analyzing, specifying, documenting, and validating business requirements to seize the new business opportunity. Typically, requirements are defined at a high level in this phase and are progressively elaborated during design and development of the solution.

  □ **Design phase.** The business analyst facilitates and collaborates in managing changes to requirements and trace requirements through design artifacts. Artifacts, abstract representations of some aspect of the to-be-built system, take multiple forms. Typical requirements artifacts include graphic models, structured models, tabular data, and structured or unstructured narratives and statements. Design artifacts may be blueprints, schematics, and design documents.

  □ **Construction phase.** The business analyst facilitates and collaborates in managing changes to requirements and tracing requirements through construction artifacts.

  □ **Test phase.** The business analyst collaborates with the test team and facilitates the user acceptance test (UAT).

  □ **Deliver phase.** The business analyst facilitates and collaborates in ensuring that the business and technical organizations are ready to accept the new business solution.

+ **Operations period**

  □ **Operation and maintenance phase.** The business analyst facilitates/collaborates in managing changes to the deployed solution to add further value to the organization.

- **Deactivate phase.** The business analyst facilitates and collaborates in determining when the solution should be replaced.

The Systems Requirements Life Cycle

The systems requirements life cycle is a collection of generally sequential project subphases involved in gathering, documenting, validating, and managing changes to business requirements. As business requirements change, changes might be needed to some or all of the business solution components. It is the business analyst who leads the requirements generation and management activities conducted within each subphase. The systems requirements subphases within each phase of the business solution life cycle are presented below, along with a brief description of the role of the business analyst at each phase.

- **Enterprise analysis**

  - **Business need.** The business analyst facilitates and collaborates in creating feasibility studies to determine the optimal solution to the problem or opportunity.

  - **Business domain scope definition.** The business analyst facilitates and collaborates in determining the scope, cost, benefit, and risk of pursuing the new opportunity.

- **Requirements**

  - **Elicitation.** The business analyst conducts interviews, administers surveys, and conducts requirements elicitation workshops to gather business requirements.

  - **Analysis.** The business analyst analyzes requirements by restating them in various forms.

- □ **Specification.** The business analyst drafts the requirements specification document and structures requirements for use.

- □ **Documentation.** The business analyst finalizes and archives the full requirements documentation set.

- □ **Validation.** The business analyst conducts structured reviews with business, technical, and management representatives.

+ **Design**

- □ **Allocate.** The business analyst develops and maintains the requirements traceability matrix to trace requirements through the design artifacts.

- □ **Mitigate risks.** The business analyst collaborates with the business and technical leads to manage risks to fulfilling requirements.

- □ **Trade-off analysis.** The business analyst collaborates with the business and technical leads to conduct trade-off analysis on high-risk requirements.

- □ **Prototype.** The business analyst collaborates with the business and technical leads to develop and review prototypes for early requirements validation.

+ **Construction**

- □ **Manage change.** The business analyst collaborates with the business and technical leads to manage changes to requirements.

- □ **Trace.** The business analyst develops and maintains the requirements traceability matrix to trace requirements through the construction artifacts.

- **Test.** The business analyst collaborates with the business and technical leads to implement corrective action when defects are discovered and leads the UAT effort.

- **Deliver.** The business analyst facilitates and collaborates in ensuring that the business and technical organizations are ready to accept the new solution by designing and implementing policies, procedures, business rules, training, manuals, retooling, staffing, and facilities.

- **Operations and maintenance phase.** The business analyst collaborates with the business and technical teams to fix problems and implement enhancements that add value to the organization.

- **Deactivate phase.** The business analyst looks toward the future—new strategies and business needs—to determine when the solution should be replaced.

The next section, Part II, describes in detail what a business analyst does in a project throughout the solution development life cycle.

Endnote

1. Hal Mooz, Kevin Forsberg, and Howard Cotterman. *Communicating Project Management: The Integrated Vocabulary of Project Management and Systems Engineering*, 2003. Hoboken, NJ: John Wiley and Sons.

Part II
The Functions of a Business Analyst

Recent studies reveal that the business analyst performs a variety of business analysis activities. The table below draws on the Evans Data Corporation research study cited in Chapter 1.[1]

Business Analysis Activities	Percent of Time
Defining the big picture—business objectives and measures of success	15
Planning and managing requirements activities and tasks	17
Eliciting requirements	16
Analyzing and documenting requirements	20
Working with other team members and users to ensure the requirements meet the business objectives	18
Communicating to the various stakeholders	14
Total	100

Part II describes the business analyst's role throughout the business solution life cycle, from strategic planning through delivery of the new solution and into operations and maintenance and finally deactivation.

Chapter 4 discusses the value strategic business analysts add when supporting the executive team in establishing strategic plans, goals, and measures of success.

Chapter 5 describes the contribution of the business analyst when the organization is analyzing potential solutions to business problems and ways to seize new business opportunities in order to achieve its strategic goals.

Chapters 6 through 8 describe the business analysis activities that take place to elicit, analyze, specify, document, validate, and manage changes to requirements throughout the project life cycle.

Chapter 9 discusses the key role of the business analyst during deployment of the new business solution and in supporting it during operations and maintenance.

Endnote

1. Evans Data Corporation. "The New Business Analyst: A Strategic Role in the Enterprise," 2006. Online at www.compuware.com/thenewstrategicBA (accessed January 2007).

Chapter 4

Strategic Planning

In This Chapter:

- Strategic Planning Overview
- Strategic Goals
- The Business Analyst's Role in Strategic Planning

Strategic Planning Overview

Strategic planning is the first phase in the business solution life cycle. During this phase, the current state of an enterprise is examined and the desired future state is determined and described by a set of broad goals. These goals are then converted to measurable objectives that must be met to achieve the strategy.

The executive management team, in its strategic planning role, defines the organization's future in terms of vision, mission, and strategic goals. Strategic planning focuses the executive team on the organization's *reason for being and future state* and provides the foundation for project investment decisions. The strategic planning process drives *portfolio management*, the business practice that selects, prioritizes, and funds change initiatives and thereby converts strategic goals into programs and supporting projects. In today's world, the strategic plan is considered a living, breathing road map that changes and evolves with business needs. Strategy changes are managed through a rigorous process so that as the strategies change, the portfolio of programs and projects is adjusted.

Strategic Goals

Scores of important goals are likely to be developed during strategic planning. Strategic goals must be converted into an organized, actionable, measurable framework to attain the results intended. To monitor the journey, executive teams now build corporate scorecards as an outgrowth of the strategic plan. Increasing the wealth of stakeholders is the ultimate goal of for-profit organizations; as a result, financial goals often rank highest. However, nonfinancial criteria should also be weighed, so that the organization invests in the future health of the enterprise. The Balanced Scorecard is a particular model that provides an effective tool to frame strategic goals.[1] In the Balanced Scorecard, goals are partitioned into four dimensions—financial, customer, internal operations, and learning and innovation—as described below.

+ *Financial* goals are the quantitative targets that address the financial outcomes of the business. Example: "Earn 6% on sales, 18% on investments, and 12% on assets this year."

+ *Customer* goals address the customer satisfaction view of the business. The primary measure is some component of customer relationships with the enterprise. Example: "Earn a customer satisfaction rating at 95% or better this year."

+ *Internal operations* goals relate to the process and operational performance and effectiveness of organizational core competencies. Measures are typically internal, comparing performance with industry benchmarks. Example: "Achieve inventory turns of 8.0 or better this year."

+ *Learning and innovation* goals address new product development, organizational learning and skill development, and application of technology and productivity tools. Example: "Increase the number of project managers with professional certification by 50%."

In the public sector, where mission results drive government agencies, the dimensions take on a slightly different slant. Measures are established to answer the following questions:

+ Customer: "How do our customers view our effectiveness?"

+ Financial: "Do we get the most cost-effective solution for the government?"

+ Internal processes: "Are our business processes effective and efficient?"

+ Innovation and improvement: "How do we continue to improve and create value for our customers?"

Just as the strategic plan is a living document, strategic goals are dynamic as well. So the process now includes tighter planning cycles to rigorously monitor progress and make course corrections along the way. The bar for adding business value is likely to be raised for every planning cycle. As always, the executive management team is ultimately accountable for setting the right strategies for the success of the organization. Today the stakes are so high that success is the only option, thus focusing more attention on the business analysis that takes place to establish strategy, goals, and resulting change initiatives.

The Business Analyst's Role in Strategic Planning

In most organizations business analysts do not contribute directly to strategic planning activities. Very senior, influential business analysts, however, might be asked to conduct market research, benchmark studies, or competitive analysis studies to provide information to the executive team as input to the strategic planning process. In some organizations, senior business analysts help plan and facilitate strategic planning sessions. Whether or not business analysts are involved in strategic planning, they should have a full understanding of the strategic direction of the enterprise to understand how new initiatives fit into the long-term strategy and/or mission of the organization and to help build and manage the business case and other relevant information regarding new project opportunities.

Business Analysts and the Strategic Planning Process

Level	Proficiency	Typical Activities
Strategic	Ability to perform strategic tasks with minimal direction	Provide support to the strategic planning team by: • Providing competitive benchmarks and organizational capability information to the executive team • Facilitating strategy sessions • Drafting and maintaining vision, mission, strategic plans, goals, and measures
Senior	Ability to perform complex tasks with minimal coaching	May provide support to the strategic business analyst by: • Participating in studies • Scribing at facilitated strategy sessions
Intermediate	Ability to perform simple to moderately complex tasks with minimal assistance	Not typically involved
Associate	Ability to perform simple tasks with assistance	Not typically involved

Please refer to *The Business Analyst as Strategist: Translating Business Strategies into Valuable Solutions*, a volume of the Business Analysis Essential Library, for an in-depth discussion of the business analyst's role in strategic planning.

Endnote

1. Robert S. Kaplan and David P. Norton. *The Balanced Scorecard: Translating a Strategy into Action*, 1996. Boston: Harvard Business School Press.

Chapter 5

Enterprise Analysis

In This Chapter:

- Enterprise Analysis Overview
- The Business Analyst's Role in Enterprise Analysis

The enterprise analysis phase of the business solution life cycle consists of the pre-project activities that depict the current and future views of the business. These views provide the information required for project selection and prioritization and for setting the direction for project work. In the enterprise analysis phase, business planning activities convert new business opportunities into new project proposals.

Enterprise Analysis Overview

Enterprise analysis begins after the executive team has developed strategic plans and goals. The core enterprise analysis activities center on:

- Identifying new business opportunities or solutions to business problems
- Conducting studies, gathering information, and determining the best business solution

- Developing a business case and decision package to submit to management so that management can decide whether to do the project, as well as the project's prioritization and funding levels

If the proposal is selected, a new project is formed and the requirements phase is entered. Enterprise analysis activities resume after the project has been completed and the benefits of the change initiative are experienced, measured, and analyzed.

An organization's ability to achieve goals through projects depends on its ability to select the most valuable projects and then execute them flawlessly. Organizational strategic alignment is achieved when strategic plans and goals are converted into a portfolio of programs and supporting projects. Strategic project leaders and core strategic project teams execute the project plans to meet objectives and deliver project outcomes, thus adding value to the enterprise. See Figure 5-1.

Figure 5-1—Organizational Strategic Alignment

The Business Analyst's Role in Enterprise Analysis

It is through the pre-project selection analysis activities that the business analyst plays a significant role in translating business strategies into proposed new business initiatives. During these early discovery and definition activities, requirements are determined and documented at a very high level. Therefore, initial requirements definition typically originates in the enterprise analysis phase of the business solution life cycle, when the product concept is first envisioned. The requirements for new business opportunities are captured in one or more initiating documents—the business case, project charter, or statement of work. All requirements should be traceable to at least one of these original sources.

There is an array of enterprise analysis activities, which are typically guided by the business analyst, leading up to project selection. Organizations use some or all of the following techniques, depending on the maturity of the organizations' enterprise analysis practices. The activities listed below appear to be sequential, but they are usually conducted concurrently and iteratively.

+ **Creating and maintaining the business architecture.** The business architecture is the set of artifacts that provide information about the business. It is a compilation of interrelated elements that depict information about the business in terms of operations; organizational structures and physical locations; the business functions and processes; business rules, policies, and procedures; and the business as a mechanism to flow value through to customers.

+ **Conducting feasibility, benchmark, and competitive analysis studies.**

  □ *A feasibility study* is an evaluation conducted to determine whether a business opportunity idea is achievable within cost, schedule, or other limitations.

▫ *A benchmark study* is a review, for the purposes of replication, of what best-of-breed organizations (often competitors) are doing to achieve their level of superior performance. It might also involve comparing the potential performance of a proposed process or product versus that of an existing product, system, or system component.

▫ *A competitive analysis study* is an evaluation of the competition in the marketplace, including past, current, and projected performance, for the purpose of establishing future plans to remain competitive.

• **Identifying new business opportunities.** As an outgrowth of strategic planning, the business analyst reviews the results of feasibility, benchmark, and competitive analysis studies, and the target business architecture, to identify potential solution alternatives to achieve strategic goals. The business analyst works with a core team of subject matter experts to identify new business opportunities and conduct trade-off analysis to determine the most viable options. The goal is to select the solution alternative that provides the most positive (valuable) outcome the fastest and poses the least risk to the enterprise.

• **Scoping and defining new business opportunities.** Once the best alternative to achieve business goals has been determined, it must be defined to the level of detail considered necessary for the portfolio planning team to make a decision whether to invest in the change initiative. This is a challenging task for the business analyst because the organization does not want to devote a significant investment to an idea that might not survive the project selection and prioritization process. Again, the business analyst works with a team of subject matter experts to compile just enough information to determine whether the proposed solution is viable.

+ **Preparing the business case for new business opportunities.** A business case should be developed for all significant change initiatives and capital projects, including major IT projects. Business unit managers might take the lead in developing business cases for projects that benefit their departments. However, many projects cross business units, and the talents of a business analyst facilitate the difficult decisions that must be made to satisfy the often-competing demands of all areas affected by the change. The business analyst brings key experts together to gain agreement on the initiative. Accurately predicting the costs and benefits of major initiatives is a critical skill that requires the combined disciplines of business analysis and project management, as well as IT expertise (to estimate the costs of software development and technology acquisition) and business prowess (to predict the business costs and value).

+ **Conducting the initial risk assessment.** Once the business case is developed, the business analyst facilitates a risk assessment session using the same set of experts. Key risks are identified and analyzed and risk responses are developed. The cost of the risk responses is estimated and an overall risk rating for the project is determined. This information is essential for the project selection and prioritization effort. Obviously, the organization strives to invest in projects that have the lowest risk, have the highest probability of success, and add the most value to the enterprise.

+ **Presenting the decision package for new business opportunities to the portfolio management team for a decision whether to fund the initiative.** *Portfolio management* is the management process embedded between *strategic planning* and *project execution*. Enterprise portfolio management involves selecting and prioritizing the portfolio of projects on the basis of strategic goals and measures. The portfolio management team is accountable for creating the right investment path for the enterprise. The quality of the decisions made by the portfolio management team is highly dependent on the information submitted to it. To enable sound decisions, the business analyst prepares the accurate, reliable, consistent, decision-support information required for the portfolio management team to understand the costs, risks, and value of proposed projects and compare their relative value to the enterprise. The business analyst typically submits the proposal to the project sponsor for approval, and then the sponsor presents it to the portfolio management team.

Many organizations with mature project management go through all the processes listed above. However, in most cases projects are funded without the rigorous business analysis that is needed to ensure that the investment is optimal. By using the business analyst to perform these strategic business analysis activities, organizations ensure that they are investing in the most valuable projects.

This overview of the enterprise analysis activities leading up to project selection and prioritization is intended to provide only a broad summary.[1] Please refer to *The Business Analyst as Strategist: Translating Business Strategies into Valuable Solutions*, a volume of the Business Analyst Essential Library, for more information.

Business Analysts and Enterprise Analysis Activities

Level	Proficiency	Typical Activities
Strategic	Ability to perform strategic tasks with minimal direction	Provide support to the portfolio management team by: • Developing and maintaining the business architecture • Defining the business problem and opportunity • Conducting feasibility studies to analyze potential solutions; identifying the best solution • Developing the business case for proposed new projects • Developing tools, processes, and policies for portfolio management • Facilitating portfolio management sessions • Measuring the value of new business solutions and comparing the value to the benefit estimate in the business case • Conducting root-cause analysis if the benefit was not obtained
Senior	Ability to perform complex tasks with minimal coaching	May provide support to the strategic business analyst by: • Participating in feasibility studies and business case development • Scribing at facilitated portfolio management sessions
Intermediate	Ability to perform simple to moderately complex tasks with minimal assistance	Not typically involved
Associate	Ability to perform simple tasks with assistance	Not typically involved

Endnote

1. Kathleen B. Hass. "From Strategy to Action: Enterprise Portfolio Management," 2005. Vienna, VA: Management Concepts, Inc.

Chapter 6

Requirements Elicitation

In This Chapter:

- What Is Elicitation?

- Prior to Elicitation

- Gathering Requirements

Business requirements are defined as the essential conditions or capabilities of the enterprise that must be supported by the business solutions. They are derived from business goals. The critical success factor in the value of the business solution after deployment is the extent to which it supports business requirements and facilitates the organization in achieving business objectives, so you must get requirements right.

During the requirements phase, the business need is elicited, analyzed, documented, and validated. Refer again to Figure 3-1 for a view of where requirements elicitation falls in the business solution life cycle.

What Is Elicitation?

Requirements elicitation is the first step in the effort to document business requirements. *Elicitation* is the process of gathering the business requirements from customers, users, and other key stakeholders. Elicitation goals include:

- Identifying the customers, users, and stakeholders to determine who should be involved in the requirements-gathering process.

- Understanding the business goals and objectives to identify the essential user tasks that support the organizational goals.

- Identifying and beginning to draft the business requirements to understand the needs of the business. This is the activity of capturing the business requirements for a target solution, as viewed by the customers, business users, and stakeholders. As the critical activities of an enterprise that must be performed to meet the organizational objectives, requirements are solution independent.

According to Karl Wiegers, requirements elicitation is no simple task:[1]

> Requirements elicitation is perhaps the most difficult, most critical, most error-prone, and most communication-intensive aspect of software development. Elicitation can succeed only through a collaborative partnership between customers and the development team. The analyst must create an environment conducive to a thorough exploration… Skill in conducting elicitation discussions comes with experience and builds on training in interviewing, group facilitation, conflict resolution, and similar activities.

Prior to Elicitation

Successful elicitation requires a considerable amount of work before the business analyst begins to actually gather requirements. Ideally, these pre-elicitation activities are led by the business analyst, who collaborates with a small core team consisting of the senior project manager, business visionary, and lead technologist. The goal of these initial activities is to understand the business opportunity, determine the scope of the effort, plan the requirements activities, and ensure participation in the effort by the appropriate stakeholders. Activities include:

+ Acquire a perspective of the needs and environment of customers, users, and stakeholders.

+ Review, or create if nonexistent, the business case, project charter, and statement of work (or similar scope definition document).

+ Understand the business vision, drivers, goals, and objectives for the new or changed business system.

+ Assemble and educate a requirements team composed of key business and technical stakeholders.

+ Further understand and document the scope of the project.

+ Define the elicitation activities to be performed and the documents and models to be produced; capture this information in the requirements management plan.

+ Plan for change throughout the business solution life cycle.

Gathering Requirements

Initial requirements discovery involves conducting requirements-gathering sessions with customers, users, and stakeholders. Requirements-gathering techniques include:

+ **Requirements elicitation workshops.** Requirements workshops are an efficient way to gather information about the business need from a diverse group of stakeholders. The advantage of bringing stakeholders together to define requirements is that conflicting and inconsistent requirement information surfaces and discrepancies are immediately resolved. Requirements are gathered quickly and collaboratively in a workshop session, linking business users with management and solution developers. A byproduct of these requirements workshops is that relationships begin to be built and a high-performing team begins to emerge.

The business analyst plays a critical role in facilitating the workshop to ensure a successful outcome, which is a difficult endeavor. Requirements workshops require a considerable amount of planning and preparation to be successful. When professional business analysis is new to an organization, it is helpful to bring in an outside facilitator. The in-house business analyst can observe the facilitation approach and focus on the discussion.

+ **Interviews.** Interviews are conducted with individuals and small groups to find out what business functions must be supported by the new solution.

+ **Surveys.** Surveys can collect a large amount of information from an array of stakeholders efficiently and quickly. They can be used to collect initial information or to test information already gathered. Valid surveys are difficult to design and administer. To mitigate the risk of gathering inaccurate information from the survey, consult with a subject matter expert to help with the survey design and information compilation.

+ **Document review.** Conduct a review of all existing documentation about the area of the business undergoing change, including policies, procedures, regulations, and process descriptions. Reviewing market data about the business process under review can also be helpful.

+ **Observation.** It is helpful to observe users conducting their day-to-day functions. This may help validate information gathered through workshops and interviews, resolve problems with requirements, and uncover missing requirements.

+ **Note-taking and feedback loops.** Hold feedback sessions with customers, users, and stakeholders to continually validate the accuracy and completeness of the requirements.

A very early iteration of the business requirements document is often the key output of these activities, in addition to any notes, diagrams, or other information captured during the elicitation sessions. Requirements are always unclear at the beginning of a project. It is through the process of progressive elaboration that requirements evolve into maturity. Hence, the nature of requirements gathering, documenting, and validating is iterative.

Business Analysts and the Requirements Elicitation Process

Level	Proficiency	Typical Activities
Strategic	Ability to perform strategic tasks with minimal direction	Not typically involved unless the project is of a critical, strategic nature
Senior	Ability to perform complex tasks with minimal coaching	*For Significant, High-Risk Projects* Planning elicitation activities and conducting elicitation sessions: + Interviews + Surveys + Workshops + Focus groups + Documentation review + Observing users in their environment

Level	Proficiency	Typical Activities
Intermediate	Ability to perform simple to moderately complex tasks with minimal assistance	*For Small to Moderate-Risk Projects* Planning elicitation activities and conducting elicitation sessions: • Interviews • Surveys • Workshops • Focus groups • Documentation review • Observing users in their environment
Associate	Ability to perform simple tasks with assistance	Provide support to intermediate and senior business analysts by scribing the information that is discovered in the elicitation sessions

See *Unearthing Business Requirements: Elicitation Tools and Techniques* for a detailed discussion of requirement elicitation and *The Art and Power of Facilitation: Running Powerful Meetings* for details on planning and conducting requirements elicitation sessions, including requirements workshops.

Endnote

1. Karl E. Wiegers. *Software Requirements: Practical Techniques for Gathering and Managing Requirements throughout the Product Development Cycle*, 2nd ed., 2003. Redmond, WA: Microsoft Press.

Chapter 7

Requirements Analysis and Specification

In This Chapter:

- Requirements Analysis

- Analysis Activities

- Requirements Specification

- Requirements Categories

Requirements analysis is the process of structuring requirements information that was gathered during elicitation into various categories, evaluating requirements for selected qualities, representing requirements in different forms, deriving detailed requirements from high-level requirements, and negotiating priorities. *Requirements specification* is the process of creating formal text documents that are elaborated from and linked to the various requirement components and categorizing and structuring the requirement components, thereby providing a repository of requirements with a completed attribute set. Refer back to Figure 3-1 for a view of where requirements analysis and specification falls in the business solution life cycle.

Requirements Analysis

Requirements analysis includes the activities needed to determine and document required function and performance characteristics, the context of implementation, stakeholder constraints and measures of effectiveness, and validation criteria. Through the analysis process, requirements are decomposed and captured in a combination of text and graphical formats. According to Scott Ambler:[1]

> The purpose of analysis is to understand what will be built, why it should be built, how much it will likely cost to build (estimation), and in what order it should be built (prioritization). This is similar to requirements elicitation, the purpose of which is to determine what your users want to have built. The main difference is that the focus of requirements gathering is on understanding your users and their potential usage of the system, whereas the focus of analysis shifts to understanding the system itself and exploring the details of the problem domain. Another way to look at analysis is that it represents the middle ground between requirements and design, the process by which your mindset shifts from what needs to be built to how it will be built.

And Karl Wiegers defines analysis as:[2]

> The process of classifying requirements information into various categories, evaluating requirements for desirable qualities, representing requirements in different forms, deriving detailed requirements from high-level requirements, negotiating priorities, and so on.

Analysis Activities

Specific analysis activities include the following:

+ *Context diagramming* to ensure that the scope of the change initiative and the boundaries of the project are fully understood by all stakeholders.

+ *Studying* requirements feasibility to determine whether the requirement is viable technically, operationally, and economically.

+ *Trading off* requirements to determine the most feasible requirement alternatives.

+ *Assessing requirement risks and constraints* and modifying requirements to mitigate identified risks. The goal is to reduce requirement risks, often through early validation prototyping techniques.

+ *Modeling* requirements to provide a visual depiction of relationships and dependencies.

+ *Prototyping* interfaces and solution subcomponents to provide a visual model of the proposed solution.

+ *Decomposing* requirements to capture business needs in enough detail for use by the solution development team.

+ *Clarifying and restating* requirements in multiple ways to ensure that they describe the real needs of the customers.

+ *Deriving* additional requirements as more is learned about the business need through the analysis activities.

+ *Prioritizing* requirements to reflect the fact that not all requirements are of equal value to the business. Prioritization is required to ensure that the most valuable features and functions are delivered to the business first.

+ *Defining terms* in a glossary or data dictionary in natural (nontechnical) language to ensure that the diverse stakeholders are truly communicating.

+ *Creating test cases* at a high level to ensure that the requirement is testable. If requirements are particularly difficult to define, it is sometimes necessary to start by designing the test that will verify that the requirement has been met and then backing into the actual requirement.

+ *Allocating* requirements to subsystems to ensure that they are satisfied by components of the system.

+ Developing *business scenarios* as a technique to ensure an understanding of requirements. A business scenario is an outline of an hypothesized chain of events. A use case is a special kind of scenario that breaks down system requirements into user functions. Each use case is a sequence of events performed by a user.

Requirements Specification

Requirements specification is complete when all the detail about a requirement is captured so that it can be included in a system specification document to be used by the solution development team. Requirements specification serves as a type of progressive elaboration, in that the requirements team often detects areas that were not defined in sufficient detail earlier. Unless these areas are addressed, they can lead to uncontrolled change to requirements. The system specification document accompanied by a database of structured requirements information is the output of the requirements specification process.

A key element of specification is identifying all the precise attributes of each unique requirement. Attributes are used for a variety of purposes, including structuring, grouping, explanation, selection, filtering, and validating. Attributes may be user-defined or system-defined. Attributes allow the requirements team to associate information with individual or related groups of requirements. In addition, the use of attributes often facilitates the requirements analysis process by enabling filtering and sorting. Typical attributes attached to requirements may include:

+ *Unique identifier* that does not change. The reference is not to be reused if the requirement is moved, changed, or deleted.

+ *Acceptance criteria* describe the nature of the test that would demonstrate to customers, end users, and stakeholders that the requirement has been met. Acceptance criteria are usually captured from the end users by asking the question: "What kind of assessment would satisfy you that this requirement has been met?"

+ *Author* of the requirement refers to who wrote it.

+ *Complexity indicator* describes how difficult the requirement will be to implement.

+ *Ownership* specifies the individual or group that needs the requirement.

+ *Performance* addresses how the requirement must be met.

+ *Priority* of the requirement rates its relative importance at a given point in time.

+ *Source* of the requirement identifies who requested it. Every requirement should originate from a source that has the authority to specify requirements.

+ *Stability indicator* is used to indicate how mature the requirement is. It is used to determine whether the requirement is firm enough to begin work on it.

+ *Status* of the requirement denotes whether it is proposed, accepted, verified with the users, or implemented.

+ *Urgency* refers to how soon the requirement is needed.

Requirements Categories

As requirements are being specified, they are categorized. Requirements are categorized into types depending on their source and applicability. Understanding requirement types helps in analyzing, structuring, and prioritizing requirements. It also enables the technical team to conduct trade-off analysis, estimate the system cost and schedule, and better assess the level of requirement changes to be expected.

Typically, requirements are broadly characterized as *functional* or *nonfunctional* (also known as *supplemental*). *Functional requirements* describe organizational capabilities the system will be able to support in terms of behaviors or operations—a specific system action or response. Functional requirements are best expressed as a verb or verb phrase. They are written so as not to unnecessarily constrain the solution, thus providing a firm foundation for the system architects.

Functional requirements look like this:

> "The solution shall provide the capability for project managers to assign contractors to work packages."

> "The solution shall notify the project manager when a task is late by more than one week."

Nonfunctional requirements stipulate a physical or performance characteristic and serve as constraints on system capabilities. Constraints pose restrictions on the acceptable solution options. Technical constraints might include the requirement to use a predetermined language or database or specific hardware. Constraints might also specify restrictions like resource utilization; message size and timing; software size; and maximum number of and size of files, records, and data elements. Technical constraints also include any enterprise architecture standards that must be followed. Business constraints include budget limitations, restrictions on the people who can do the work, and skill sets available. As previously mentioned, business rules define the constraints to business processes that must be followed.

Nonfunctional requirements look like this:

"The response time for rescheduling the tasks shall be no more than ten seconds."

"The solution shall be compatible with Microsoft Office 2002."

Business Analysts and the Analysis and Specification Processes

Level	Proficiency	Typical Activities
Strategic	Ability to perform strategic tasks with minimal direction	Not typically involved unless the project is of a critical, strategic nature
Senior	Ability to perform complex tasks with minimal coaching	*For Significant, High-Risk Projects* • Construct complex models—process, data, work flow, object-oriented, use cases, functional decomposition, diagrams, etc. • Develop business architecture: as-is/to-be models • Analyze and manage requirement risk • Structure requirements for traceability • Prioritize requirements • Draft requirements specifications
Intermediate	Ability to perform simple to moderately complex tasks with minimal assistance	*For Small to Moderate-Risk Projects* • Construct complex models—process, data, work flow, object-oriented, use cases, functional decomposition diagrams, etc. • Develop business architecture: as-is/to-be models • Analyze and manage requirement risk • Structure requirements for traceability • Prioritize requirements • Draft requirements specifications
Associate	Ability to perform simple tasks with assistance	Provide support to intermediate and senior business analysts by scribing the information as requirements are analyzed and specificed

Endnotes

1. Scott W. Ambler. *When Does(n't) Agile Modeling Make Sense?* Online at www.agilemodeling.com/essays/whenDoesAMWork.htm (accessed April 8, 2005).

2. Karl E. Wiegers. *Software Requirements: Practical Techniques for Gathering and Managing Requirements throughout the Product Development Cycle,* 2nd ed., 2003. Redmond, WA: Microsoft Press.

Chapter 8

Requirements Documentation, Validation, and Management

In This Chapter:

- Good Requirements Documentation

- Requirements Validation

- Requirements Management

After analysis and specification (Chapter 7), the next step is to finalize the full set of requirements documentation, consisting of all the artifacts that are used to state requirements (lists, tables, models, and text statements and documents). After the final documentation set is created, the project team, led by the business analyst, examines the requirements and validates them, meaning that the team confirms the requirements are up to date and accurately reflect all the collected information about the business solution to be built, its stakeholders, and the organization. Following the core project team review, there is usually a series of reviews by the major stakeholder groups, both business and technical. After requirements have been validated and approval is secured to move into design and construction, the requirements changes must be managed, as requirements are constantly examined and improved based on the progress of the project.

Refer back to Figure 3-1 for a view of where requirements documentation, initial validation, and management fall in the business solution life cycle.

Good Requirements Documentation

As the business analyst approaches the end of the requirements phase, final documentation is produced. Text documentation is a significant component of virtually all requirements artifacts. Therefore, it is imperative that the business analyst be able to write requirement statements that are easily understood.

Requirements documentation must be clear, concise, and stated in natural language because it is used by virtually everyone associated with the project. Selected types of requirements, like regulatory mandates, safety standards, and security requirements, might need to be expressed formally using scientific or technical language. This is allowed, as long as they are mapped back to the business requirements that are more easily understood. In most cases, however, the language used to document business requirements should be as simple and straightforward as possible.

A diagram can express structure and relationships more clearly than text can. For precise definition of concepts, however, clearly articulated language is better than diagrams. Therefore, both text and graphics are essential for a complete set of requirements. Transforming graphical requirements into text form can make them more understandable to nontechnical members of the team. Good requirements should be:

- **Feasible.** The requirements must be technically, economically, and operationally possible.

- **Necessary.** The requirements must represent the real needs of the organization.

+ **Prioritized.** The requirements must be ranked according to the value of the function or feature to the organization.

+ **Unambiguous.** The requirements must be clear so that they will be interpreted consistently across stakeholder groups.

+ **Complete.** The requirements must represent all the functions and features needed to meet the business objectives.

+ **Verifiable.** The requirements must be testable.

+ **Consistent.** The requirements must be in harmony with one another and must not contradict each other.

+ **Correct.** The requirements must accurately represent business functions and adhere to business rules.

+ **Modifiable.** The requirements must be flexible so that they can be adapted to changing business needs.

+ **Traceable.** The requirements must be structured so that they can be traced to hardware, software, test cases, training manuals, and documentation artifacts throughout the solution development life cycle.

+ **Usable after development.** The requirements must be detailed enough to support maintaining and enhancing the business system during the operations and maintenance phase of the business solution life cycle.

Requirements Validation

Requirements validation is the process of evaluating requirement documents, models, and attributes to determine whether they satisfy the business needs and are complete to the point that the technical team can begin working on system design and development. The set of requirements is compared to the original initiating documents (e.g., business case, project charter, or statement of work) to ensure completeness.

Beyond establishing completeness, validation activities include evaluating requirements from a technical standpoint to ensure that design risks associated with the requirements are minimized before further investment is made in system development. Validation techniques include document reviews, product demonstrations, prototyping, and, finally, user acceptance testing. It should be noted that the process of validating requirements typically requires substantial time and effort because stakeholders might have different expertise, perspectives, and expectations.

Requirements Management

A set of phase exit activities occurs upon completing the requirements phase and transitioning to solution design and construction. Phase exit activities involve presenting requirements for review and approval at a formal control gate review session, a structured review that accepts the requirements and authorizes the project to continue.

At this point, the business analyst and project manager update the project schedule, cost, and scope estimates and the business case to provide the salient information needed to determine whether continued investment in the project is warranted. For organizations that have a mature portfolio management process in place, the current state of the project is presented to the portfolio management team to secure funding to proceed. Upon securing approval to proceed, the business analyst transitions into requirements management activities and the project manager transitions into detailed planning for the design, construction, test, delivery, and operations and maintenance of the new business solution.

Requirements management involves tracking and coordinating requirements allocation, status, and change activities throughout the rest of the business solution life cycle. In addition to managing changes to requirements, the business analyst and project manager collaboratively manage the relationship between the product scope, which is the features and functions that characterize a product, service, or result, and the project scope, which is the work that must be performed to deliver a product, service, or result within the specified features and functions. Requirements management activities include:

+ *Allocating* (or *partitioning*) requirements to different subsystems or subcomponents of the system. Top-level requirements are allocated to components defined in the system architecture, such as hardware, software, manual procedures, and training.

+ *Tracing* requirements throughout system design and development to track where in the system each requirement is satisfied. As requirements are converted to design documentation, the sets of requirements documentation, models, specifications, and designs must be rigorously linked to ensure that the relevant business needs are satisfied.

+ *Managing changes* and enhancements to the system. Managing requirements involves being able to add, delete, and modify requirements during all phases of the business solution life cycle.

+ *Validating and verifying* requirements. The business analyst continues to facilitate the validation and verification of requirements throughout the life of the project. The purpose of verification and validation is to ensure that the system satisfies the requirements, as well as the specifications and conditions imposed on it by those requirements. Validation provides evidence that the designed solution satisfies the requirements through user involvement in testing, demonstration, and other inspection techniques. The final validation step is the user acceptance testing, led and facilitated by the business analyst. Verification provides evidence that the designed solution satisfies the requirements specification through test, inspection, demonstration, and/or analysis.

Business Analysts and the Documentation, Validation, and Requirements Management Processes

Level	Proficiency	Typical Activities
Strategic	Ability to perform strategic tasks with minimal direction	Not typically involved unless the project is of a critical, strategic nature
Senior	Ability to perform complex tasks with minimal coaching	*For Significant, High-Risk Projects* • Finalize the requirements artifact set • Plan and conduct structured quality reviews of requirements and solutions • Develop test plans • Provide support to the technical team • Manage user acceptance test activities • Manage changes to requirements
Intermediate	Ability to perform simple to moderately complex tasks with minimal assistance	*For Small to Moderate-Risk Projects* • Finalize the requirements artifact set • Plan and conduct structured quality reviews of requirements and solutions • Develop test plans • Provide support to the technical team • Manage user acceptance test activities • Manage changes to requirements
Associate	Ability to perform simple tasks with assistance	Provide support to intermediate and senior business analysts by helping finalize the artifact set

Chapter 9

Business Solution Delivery, Operation, and Maintenance

In This Chapter:

- Business Solution Delivery

- Managing Change

- Business Solution Maintenance and Enhancement

Although the requirements have been properly documented, validated, and managed, the business analyst's job is still not done. The business analyst must lead the effort to prepare the organization for the final deliverable of the product and is also involved in ongoing operations and maintenance once the new business solution is operational. Once again, refer to Figure 3-1 to see where these activities fall in the business solution life cycle.

Business Solution Delivery

Planning for the organizational change brought about by the delivery of a major new business solution is often partially or even completely overlooked by project teams that are focused solely on the IT system development and implementation. While the technical members of the project team plan and support the implementation of the new application system into the IT production environment, the business analyst works with management of the business units undergoing change to bring about the benefits expected of the new business solution. The business analyst and business unit management:

- Assess the organizational readiness for change; plan and implement a cultural change program

- Assess the current state of the knowledge and skills resident within the business; determine the knowledge and skills needed to optimize the new business solution; and plan for and support the training, retooling, and staff acquisition needed to fill skill gaps

- Assess the current state of the organizational structure within the business domain; determine the organizational structure needed to optimize the new business solution; plan for and support the organizational restructuring

- Develop and implement a robust communication campaign to support the organizational change initiative

- Determine management's role in championing the change and enlist and support management to fill that role

Managing Change

There are many cultural and physical barriers to adopting a major new business solution. The business leadership might have too many conflicting and demanding priorities. The physical facilities needed to support the new business solution might not be well understood. The users—the actual operators of the new IT system and new business processes—might not have the knowledge and skills needed to optimally use the new technology. The senior leadership of the organization may be reluctant to be actively involved because they might not see modeling and teaching the new practices as their role.

Overcoming barriers to cultural change might involve major shifts in the current vision and skills resident in the organization. The business analyst employs many strategies for making change work, including:[1]

+ Working with the leadership team to create a climate in which change can succeed

+ Enlisting formal and informal leaders within the organization to drive the change

+ Ensuring there is clear ownership and accountability within the business unit(s) for maintaining and improving the quality of the new business process and IT systems

+ Focusing on and communicating improvements early in the deployment

+ Providing role-modeling, mentoring, and coaching to reinforce new business practices

+ Implementing reward and recognition systems that are aligned with the new business practices

+ Reacting to critical incidents with the new business solution quickly

+ Recognizing and addressing stress and resistance associated with culture change

+ Employing strategies to sustain culture change, including:

  □ Using coaching and mentoring programs

  □ Permanently linking rewards to the use of new business practices

□ Placing equal emphasis on all aspects of the business system, including customer satisfaction, profit, employee satisfaction, continuous learning, process efficiency, and driving value through the organization to the customer

Business Solution Maintenance and Enhancement

The business analyst's contribution to the success of the project does not end when the business solution is delivered and operational. The business analyst maintains key responsibilities during the operations and maintenance (O&M) phase of the business solution life cycle. The business analyst provides maintenance services to prevent and correct defects in the business solution. The defects could be problems with the IT system (e.g., inaccurate data, application defects, technical infrastructure inadequacies) or issues within the business process (e.g., procedure inefficiencies, information gaps, skill gaps).

Measuring Customer Satisfaction and Solution Value

Typical documentation produced and reviewed by the business analyst in this phase includes process efficiency measures, customer satisfaction indicators, system validation procedures, system validation reports, maintenance reports, annual operational reports, and deactivation plan and procedures. In addition, the business analyst plays a vital role in determining if the new solution delivered the expected benefits predicted in the business case. If the expected benefits are not attained, the business analyst conducts root-cause analysis to determine if the investment decision was flawed, or if the project was not executed optimally and, therefore, increased the cost of building the new solution.

Resolving Problems and Managing Enhancements

The business analyst also plays a major role in resolving problems and managing enhancements to the system and in determining when the system should be replaced and therefore deactivated. *Enhancements* are defined as changes that increase the value provided by the system to the business. Clearly, if requested enhancements cost more to implement than the value provided to the business, they are not cost-effective. It is the business analyst who continues to examine the value that the proposed functions and features will bring about and who compares the value to the cost to develop and operate the new system components.

Business Analysts and the Delivery and Operations and Maintenance Processes

Level	Proficiency	Typical Activities
Strategic	Ability to perform strategic tasks with minimal direction	Not typically involved unless the project is of a critical, strategic nature
Senior	Ability to perform complex tasks with minimal coaching	*For Significant, High-Risk Projects* ◆ Manage customer acceptance of new business solutions ◆ Analyze help desk requests ◆ Conduct root-cause analysis of problems ◆ Plan and implement continuous improvement of the solution ◆ Administer customer satisfaction surveys ◆ Measure the value of new business solutions and compare to benefit estimate in business case ◆ Conduct root-cause analysis if the benefit was not obtained

Level	Proficiency	Typical Activities
Interme-diate	Ability to perform simple to moderately complex tasks with minimal assistance	*For Small to Moderate-Risk Projects* • Manage customer acceptance of new business solutions • Analyze help desk requests • Conduct root-cause analysis of problems • Plan and implement continuous improvement of the solution • Administer customer satisfaction surveys • Measure the value of new business solutions and compare to benefit estimate in business case • Conduct root-cause analysis if the benefit was not obtained
Associate	Ability to perform simple tasks with assistance	Provide support to intermediate and senior business analysts by helping fulfill help desk requests and solve problems

Endnote

1. Rita Chao Hadden. *Leading Culture Change in Your Software Organizations: Delivering Results Early,* 2003. Vienna, VA: Management Concepts, Inc.

Part III
Other Considerations

This section provides additional information for the business analyst to consider while conducting business analysis activities. In Chapter 10, we present general requirements engineering best practices and contemporary approaches to improving requirements management and project performance.

In Chapter 11, we discuss the complex array of knowledge and skills needed to successfully perform business analyst activities and present a path for the professional development of business analysts.

In Chapter 12, we present a business analysis maturity model that can guide organizations as they embark on the journey of building professional business analysis capabilities.

Chapter 10

Requirements Engineering Considerations

In This Chapter:

- Agile Development
- Iteration
- Scalability

To understate the obvious, requirements engineering is a difficult and risky business. Ideally, we would get a clear and thorough picture of the requirements before development, obtain customer sign-off on these requirements, and then set up procedures that limit requirements changes following sign-off. However, regardless of the care taken in requirements engineering, requirements are going to change due to several circumstances:

- ✦ The business environment is dynamic. In today's economy, fundamental business forces are rapidly changing the value of system features. What might be a good set of requirements now may not be good in a few months or a year.

- ✦ Everything in IT systems development depends on the requirements. The assumption that fixed requirements are not the norm also means the original plan is subject to change.

+ Estimation is difficult for IT projects because they are basically unique endeavors, similar to research and development projects. The nature of IT systems is intangible, and the real value is difficult to predict.

Keeping in mind the difficulty in defining and managing business requirements, and having described business analysis practices earlier in this book, it is imperative that we discuss three additional concepts relating to *how* we implement business analysis techniques: *agile development*, the *iterative* nature of requirements generation and system development (especially for software-intensive systems), and *scalability*.

Agile Development

Over the past few years, there's been a rapidly growing interest in agile (or *lightweight*) methodologies. Described as an approach that rids IT development of burdensome bureaucracy or, alternatively, as a license to hack, agile methods have generated interest throughout the IT world. The emphasis of agile methods differs substantially from the emphasis of traditional, heavyweight engineering methods. The most notable divergence is that agile methods are less document-oriented; they usually emphasize using a minimal amount of documentation for a given task. Moreover, agile methods often spotlight source code as a key part of documentation. There are two other fundamental distinctions between agile and traditional project management: [1]

+ **Agile methods are adaptive rather than predictive.** Engineering and project management methods plan out a large part of the solution in great detail and then manage changes throughout the project. Agile methods attempt to adapt and thrive on change.

+ **Agile methods are people-oriented rather than process-oriented.** The goal of engineering methods is to define a process that is repeatable and independent of the composition of the project team. Agile methods focus on the skill of the development team. They try to make the process more tightly support the team in its work.

The world of agile analysis challenges business analysts to become the communication mentors and coaches of project teams. For this to happen, one of the tenets of agile development must be followed: active stakeholder participation must occur throughout the project life cycle. Instead of requirements elicitation sessions and interviews to find out what customers want, real-time working sessions with IT system developers take place that help the customer determine what it wants and needs.

The obvious enabler to active stakeholder participation is co-location of the business and development team. However, the business side cannot always free critical resources to work with the development team on a full-time basis. In this case, the business analyst, as usual, conducts interviews and workshops with the business people in their own environment, with key members of the development team present to hear "the voice of the customer."

What is agile analysis? The business analyst follows the same practices outlined above, while incorporating these characteristics. [2]

+ Agile analysis is *communication rich*, valuing face-to-face meetings and teleconferencing over documentation and e-mail.

+ Agile analysis is *highly iterative*. Analysis and design activities are dependent on each other and in practice are conducted in an iterative manner. Indeed, since estimating is part of analysis, estimating the cost of a solution without knowing the solution design is impossible.

+ Agile analysis is *highly incremental*, so that components of the solution can be implemented for customer feedback before committing to further investment in development. This approach facilitates trade-off analysis and critical decision-making on the part of the customer.

+ Agile analysis follows the premise that *good is good enough*. It is the art of applying just the right amount of rigor, and resisting over-engineering the solution—the motto is *barely sufficient is enough to move forward*.

Ambler presents this definition of agile analysis:[3]

> Agile analysis is a highly iterative and incremental process where developers and project stakeholders actively work together to understand the domain, to identify what needs to be built, to estimate that functionality, to prioritize the functionality, and in the process, optionally producing artifacts that are just barely good enough.

When is it appropriate to use agile methods? Current thinking suggests that these methods should be used when the following conditions are present. The absence of one or more of these circumstances will likely put the agile approach at risk:[4]

+ **Your organization is transitioning to more rigor.** If your IT development team has been following the code-and-fix method, switching to agile methods will apply some discipline to the process. The agile approach has the advantage of being easier to implement than a more rigorous approach. Much of the advantage of agile methods stems from their light weight. When little or no process has been employed in the past, simpler processes are more likely to be followed than complex processes.

+ **You use small core teams.** The development team must be small, colocated, high-performing, dedicated full-time, highly skilled, and empowered to make most project decisions.

+ **Requirements are unknown.** Agile approaches are appropriate when requirements are uncertain or volatile. Logic dictates that if requirements are unstable, you cannot have a stable design or rigidly adhere to a planned process.

+ **Stakeholders are highly invested.** It is important for the customer to understand that when requirements change, following a predictive process is risky. In addition, the customer must be willing to be involved during the entire development process.

+ **You use incremental development.** Agile methods work well when you are building the solution incrementally.

Iteration

Although the steps in the business analysis process appear to be sequential, they are unquestionably performed iteratively. Iterating is the best defense when attempting to control an unpredictable process. The business analyst needs to build in candid feedback mechanisms at frequent intervals to reveal the status of requirements and development. The key to this feedback is an iterative approach to requirements generation and solution design.

Whether the method is called incremental, evolutionary, staged, or spiral, the techniques are iterative in nature. Early prototypes are produced; these are followed by incremental working versions that contain a subset of the required features. These working subsystems possess limited functionality, but are otherwise true to system requirements. The value of iterative development is in regular customer reviews and feedback following each iteration.

The best validation that requirements have been met is a tested, integrated system. Documents and models often contain undetected defects. When users actually work with a system, flaws, whether caused by a system defect or a misunderstood requirement, become evident.

For the project manager, a new approach to planning is essential. Rolling wave planning is the order of the day. In rolling wave planning, short-term plans cover a single iteration and are quite detailed, while later iterations are planned at only a high level. Iterative development provides a firm foundation in each increment, which becomes the basis of later waves of plans.

Iterative, agile, incremental development is the latest tool for building business and IT project achievement. Results can be dramatic. Business value is delivered faster and cheaper. Customers see constant progress. Frequent feedback keeps the project aligned with business needs, since flexibility and change are built into the project. Value-based prioritization ensures that the most important features of the solution are delivered first. Feedback is the key: it's about learning faster, not working faster.

Scalability

All the activities discussed in Part II of this book are performed whether a light or heavy methodology is used. They are likely to be executed in a broad sense at project initiation, and progressively elaborated as the project traverses its life cycle. For small, straightforward projects that are easily understood, a minimal amount of requirements documentation is appropriate. Indeed, the rule is that the smaller the team, the less formal the documentation. However, for significant, complex, high-risk projects, a full set of approved requirements documentation is in order. For low- to moderate-risk projects, the rigor should be scaled appropriately, with more formality and structure in the higher risk areas of the project. Refer to

Figure 10-1. This model helps diagnose the risk and complexity of a project and, therefore, helps to determine the amount of rigor to apply to project and requirements management.

Figure 10-1—Project Complexity Model

	Project Profile		
Complexity Dimensions	Small Independent Low Risk	Medium Moderately Complex Some Risk	Large Highly Complex Significant Risk
Time/Cost	<3 months <$250K	3–6 months $250K–$750K	>6 months >$750K
Team Size	3–4 team members	5–10 team members	>10 team members
Team Composition	Team staffed internally	Team staffed with some internal and some external resources	Complex team structure, e.g., contractor teams, virtual teams, culturally diverse teams, outsourced teams
Competing Demands	Schedule, budget, and scope are flexible	Schedule, budget, and scope can undergo minor variations, but deadlines are firm	Deadline is fixed and cannot be changed; schedule, budget, scope, and quality have no room for flexibility
Problem and Solution Clarity	Easily understood problem and solution; solution is readily achievable using existing technologies	Either problem is difficult to understand, the solution is unclear or difficult to achieve, or the technology is new to the organization	Both problem and solution are difficult to define or understand, solution is difficult to achieve, and solution likely to be using unproven or complex technologies
Stability of Requirements	Requirements understood, straightforward, and stable	Requirements undestood, but are expected to change	Requirements are poorly understood and largely undefined
Strategic Importance Political Implications Multiple Stakeholders	No political implications	Some direct mission impact, minor political implications, 2–3 stakeholder groups	Affects core mission and has major political implications; visible at highest levels of the organization, multiple stakeholder groups with conflicting expectations
Level of Change	Impacts a single business unit	Impacts a number of business units	Large-scale organizational change that impacts enterprise, spans functional groups or agencies, shifts or transforms the organization

Significant Risk	Moderate Risk	Low Risk
Level of change is enterprise, or two or more categories are in the large column.	Four or more categories are in the medium column; or one category is in the large column and three or more are in the medium column.	Remaining combinations

See *From Analyst to Leader: Elevating the Role of the Business Analyst* for more information on using the complexity model to manage challenging projects.

Endnotes

1. Martin Fowler. *The New Methodology*, 2003. Online at www.martinfowler.com/articles/newMethodology.html (accessed April 8, 2005).

2. Scott W. Ambler. *Agile Analysis*. Online at www.agilemodeling.com/essays/agileAnalysis.htm (accessed April 8, 2005).

3. ibid.

4. ibid.

Chapter 11

The Grooming of the Business Analyst

In This Chapter:

- A Complex Array of Skills and Knowledge
- Mapping Out Your Business Analyst Development Program
- Business Analysis Challenges

How do organizations develop the exceptional business analysts needed to bridge the chasm between the business and technical communities? As with any other leadership role, competency comes from acquiring education and training, seeking mentoring and coaching, and jumping in head first to learn the discipline.

A Complex Array of Skills and Knowledge

The role of the business analyst requires leadership skills as well as business and technical expertise. Formal qualifications include studies of computing and management information systems, coupled with traditional business administration and leadership courses. Individuals seeking to acquire business analyst education, training, and real-world experience should focus on the following areas:[1]

- The overall requirements generation process
  - Requirements initiation

- □ Systems requirements elicitation
- □ Requirement types
- □ How to write good requirements
- ◆ Documenting requirements
  - □ Requirements definition
  - □ System requirements documentation
- ◆ Requirements feasibility and reliability
  - □ Cost/benefit analysis
  - □ Alternative solution analysis
  - □ Feasibility and reliability risk analysis
- ◆ Managing system requirements
  - □ Tools and techniques
  - □ Technical specifications
  - □ Test plans
  - □ Requirements traceability process
  - □ Requirements and system development
  - □ Requirements and systems engineering processes
- ◆ Systems engineering planning
  - □ Requirements management controls
  - □ Requirements analysis for IT systems
  - □ Requirements functional analysis and allocation

▫ Requirements and systems design

▫ Requirements and systems implementation

Mapping Out Your Business Analyst Development Program

Enlightened organizations in both the public and private sectors are creating cohesive career management plans for business analysts to develop their potential, match their skills to assignments, track performance, and reward them appropriately. Components of world-class, professional business analysis career programs include most of these elements: mentoring and on-the-job training; advancement based on education, testing, and experience; defined evaluation and compensation processes; suitable titles and advancement opportunities; and formal off-the-shelf and customized training.

When it comes to training, look for leading-edge business analysis training offerings focused on increased performance, best practices, and project results. The courses should be based on sound systems engineering principles; focused on leadership and facilitation skills; rich in lean thinking, agile tool sets; targeted toward real-world IT situations, and filled with tailoring techniques for small, medium, and large high-risk projects. The course offerings should be designed to provide practical guidelines and skills that lead to immediate improvements in writing, defining, analyzing, and managing business requirements.

Whether you are a person developing your career or a manager advancing your organization's IT business analysis capability, select education and mentoring offerings that increase the value your projects contribute through contemporary business analysis approaches. Seek consultants who will work with you to select the best mix of courses and reinforcement strategies.

Figure 11-1 presents additional information on creating a business analyst development program by mapping competencies to career level.

Figure 11-1—Business Analyst
Career Path with Competency Requirements

Level	Proficiency	Responsibilities	Competency Requirements
Strategic	Ability to perform strategic tasks with minimal direction	**Strategic Planning** • Provide competitive information to the executive team • Facilitate strategy sessions • Draft and maintain strategic plans, goals, and measures **Enterprise Analysis** • Develop and maintain the business architecture • Define business problems and opportunities • Conduct feasibility studies to analyze potential solutions; identify optimal solution • Develop the business case for proposed new projects • Develop tools, processes, and policies for portfolio management • Facilitate portfolio management sessions • Measure the value of new business solutions and compare to benefit estimate in business case • Conduct root-cause analysis if the benefit was not obtained **Mentor Senior-Level BAs**	• Strategic and business planning and management • Business domain knowledge • Technology as competitive advantage • Business outcome thinking • Management of power and politics • Project, program, and portfolio management • Systems engineering and business analysis principles and techniques • Enterprise and business architecture • Financial management and business case development • Market research, creativity, innovation • Business process reengineering • Six Sigma • Organizational change management • Communication to executives • Problem solving, negotiation, decision making • Facilitation and meeting management • Authenticity, ethics, integrity • Customer relationship management • Coaching and mentoring • Team building and leadership

Level	Proficiency	Responsibilities	Competency Requirements
Senior	Ability to perform complex tasks with minimal coaching	*For Significant High-Risk Projects* **Elicit Requirements** • Conduct elicitation sessions: interviews, surveys, focus groups, workshops **Analyze and Specify Requirements** • Construct complex models—process, data, workflow, object-oriented, use cases, functional decomposition diagrams, etc. • Develop business architecture: as-is and to-be models • Analyze and manage requirement risk • Structure requirements for traceability • Prioritize requirements • Draft requirement specifications **Document, Validate, and Manage Requirements** • Finalize the requirements artifact set • Plan and conduct structured quality reviews of requirements and solutions • Develop test plans • Support technical team • Manage user acceptance test activities • Manage changes to requirements **Solution Delivery, O&M** • Manage customer acceptance of new business solutions • Analyze helpdesk requests • Conduct root-cause analysis of problems • Plan and implement continuous improvement of the solution • Administer customer satisfaction surveys • Measure the value of new business solutions and compare to benefit estimate in business case • Conduct root-cause analysis if the benefit was not obtained **Mentor Intermediate-Level BAs**	• Business domain knowledge • Technology as competitive advantage • Business outcome thinking • Management of power and politics • Project and program management • Systems engineering • Advanced business analysis principles and techniques, e.g., complex modeling, verification, and validation • Requirements risk management • Enterprise and business architecture • Financial management and business case development • Creativity and innovation • Business process reengineering • Six Sigma • Organizational change management • Communication to business and technical teams • Problem solving, negotiation, decision making • Facilitation and meeting management • Authenticity, ethics, integrity • Customer relationship management • Coaching and mentoring • Team building and leadership

Level	Proficiency	Responsibilities	Competency Requirements
Interme-diate	Ability to perform simple to moderately complex tasks with minimal assistance	**For Small to Moderate–Risk Projects** **Elicit Requirements** • Conduct elicitation sessions: interviews, surveys, focus groups, workshops **Analyze and Specify Requirements** • Construct models—process, data, workflow, object-oriented, use-cases, functional decomposition diagrams, etc. • Develop business architecture: as-is and to-be models • Analyze and manage requirement risk • Structure requirements for traceability • Prioritize requirements • Draft requirement specifications **Document, Validate, and Manage Requirements** • Finalize the requirements artifact set • Plan and conduct structured quality reviews of requirements and solutions • Develop test plans • Support technical team • Manage User Acceptance Test activities • Manage changes to requirements **Solution Delivery, O&M** • Manage customer acceptance of new business solutions • Analyze help desk requests • Conduct root-cause analysis of problems • Plan and implement continuous improvement of the solution • Administer customer satisfaction surveys • Measure the value of new business solutions and compare to benefit estimate in business case • Conduct root-cause analysis if the benefit was not obtained **Mentor Junior-Level BAs**	• Business domain knowledge • Technology as competitive advantage • Project management • Systems engineering • Business analysis principles and techniques, e.g., modeling, verification, and validation • Requirements risk management • Business architecture • Financial management and business case management • Creativity and innovation • Business process reengineering • Six Sigma • Organizational change management • Communication to business and technical teams • Problem solving, negotiation, decision making • Facilitation and meeting management • Authenticity, ethics, integrity • Customer relationship management • Coaching and mentoring • Team building and leadership

Level	Proficiency	Responsibilities	Competency Requirements
Associate	Ability to perform simple tasks with assistance	Support Intermediate and Senior BAs • Review and compile results of interviews and surveys • Scribe interview notes and workshop output • Build simple models • Provide support for the help desk	• Project management principles • Business analysis principles • Business process reengineering principles • Six Sigma principles • Business writing • Problem solving • Authenticity, ethics, integrity • Team versus individual performance

Business Analysis Challenges

Business analysts should be taught to avoid these pitfalls at all costs:

+ **Acting as a barrier.** Business analysts sometimes assume too much influence over project decisions. Some business analysts may stand between the technical and business communities as a barrier, instead of serving as a facilitator and enabler and bringing the technical and business communities together at the table.

+ **Possessing lagging business and technical acumen.** Maintaining credibility with both the technical and business communities requires staying current with technology advances and business trends.

+ **Creating analysis paralysis.** Business analysts are often tempted to overanalyze. They may stretch out the analysis period rather than move on to iterating. Several iterations, with feedback from both the business and technical communities, are more effective than a single, all-encompassing analysis effort. Sometimes overanalyzing leads the business analyst to make promises based on theoretical models that may not work in practice.

Endnote

1. Jag Sodhi and Prince Sodhi. *Managing IT Systems Requirements*, 2003. Vienna, VA: Management Concepts, Inc.

Chapter 12

A Business Analysis Maturity Model

In This Chapter:

- Introducing the CompassBA/PM™ Organizational Maturity Model

- Skipping Maturity Levels

- The Levels of the CompassBA/PM™ Organizational Maturity Model

How do organizations go about building mature business analysis capabilities? How do they determine:

+ How their business analysis practices can enable them to achieve even higher levels of profit (or better achieve their mission) and meet their strategic goals and objectives?

+ Their strengths and weaknesses in business analysis?

+ What areas they need to concentrate on so that they can immediately increase project success?

+ Whether they need to change their existing practices, add new tools and technologies, or provide additional training for their staff?

+ How they can best serve their business customers and attain both project and organizational success?

Part of the way businesses can determine answers to these questions is to use organizational maturity assessments, which are powerful tools for improving overall project performance. Using a business analysis maturity model and conducting a maturity assessment provide an organization with a framework to use when implementing new capabilities and evaluating progress. The assessment helps an organization understand its current capabilities, establish a capability baseline, identify appropriate areas for improvement, select high-priority improvement actions, and build organizational readiness to change.

An organizational maturity assessment provides a roadmap for improvement based on the current state of the organization's unique strengths and weaknesses. Its benefit is in narrowing the scope of improvement activities to those key practices that provide the next foundational level for extending the organization's current business analysis capabilities. Assessment team members also provide a recommended-action plan for implementing the high-priority recommendations.

Introducing the Compass BA/PM™ Organizational Maturity Model

The CompassBA/PM™ Organizational Maturity Model is a staged maturity model similar to those used by several standard-setting bodies. The model presented here is unique because of its distinctive, integrated view. The model is designed specifically for organizations whose competitive advantage is linked to their ability to rapidly deploy business solutions with a major IT component and to change those systems as the business need evolves. The CompassBA/PM™ Organizational Maturity Model (OMM) is targeted toward organizations that are dependent on successful IT projects. It integrates business analysis, project management, and systems engineering practices. Refer to Figure 12-1, the CompassBA/PM™ Organizational Maturity Model, which was developed by Kathleen

B. Hass and is used by Management Concepts in its consulting practice.

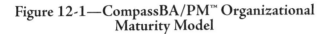

Figure 12-1—CompassBA/PM™ Organizational
Maturity Model

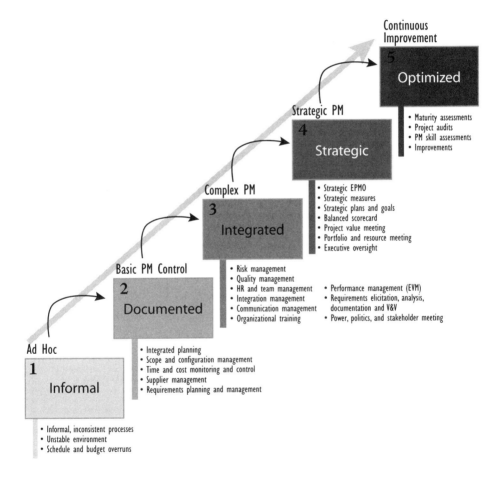

The CompassBA/PM™ OMM adheres to the proven concepts for effective change, focusing those aspects on improving the three key IT capabilities—project management, business analysis, and systems engineering.

CompassBA/PM™ OMM is mapped to industry standards by establishing specific business analysis, project management, and software engineering practice goals to be achieved to reach advanced levels of the model. The power of the CompassBA/PM™ OMM comes from the integration of:

+ The project management knowledge areas described in the Project Management Institute's (PMI®) *A Guide to the Project Management Body of Knowledge (PMBOK® Guide)*, third edition, and the areas of project management defined by the *PMBOK® Guide's* knowledge requirements and described in terms of the component processes, practices, inputs, outputs, tools, and techniques contained therein

+ The key practices embodied in the International Institute of Business Analysis' (IIBA) *Business Analysis Body of Knowledge (BABOK™ Guide)*, draft version 2.0, described in terms of key practices and techniques

+ The SEI Capability Maturity Model® Integrated (CMMI®) process areas for systems engineering, software engineering, integrated product and process development, and supplier sourcing, which represent a group of best practices that, when performed collectively, satisfy a set of goals considered important for making significant improvement in that area

The CompassBA/PM™ OMM describes the key elements of a fully effective project, program, and portfolio management environment, achieving a strategic focus at higher levels of the model. These elements are used in the assessment process for both benchmarking and evaluation. By considering the presence or absence of these elements, an organization can determine a ranking of 1 to 5 for the maturity of strategic business practices. The established ranking scale provides plateaus for the purpose of continuous improvement of project delivery capability.

The five-level scale is common for maturity models. Thus, maturity ratings can be compared across industries or even across models. Higher maturity levels are directly correlated to more effective procedures; higher-quality deliverables; lower project costs; higher project team morale; a better balance between cost, schedule, and scope; and, ultimately, improved profits for the organization.[1] The staged maturity model was chosen because it:[2]

+ Provides a proven sequence of improvements, beginning with basic management practices and progressing through a predefined and proven path of successive levels, each serving as a foundation for the next

+ Permits comparisons across and among organizations by using maturity levels

+ Provides a single rating that summarizes appraisal results and allows comparisons among organizations

Skipping Maturity Levels

The CompassBA/PM™ OMM identifies the levels through which an organization should traverse to establish a culture of project success. Because each maturity level of the CompassBA/PM™ OMM forms a necessary foundation on which to build the next level of practices, trying to skip levels can be counterproductive and often leads to diminished returns on the process improvement investment.

That said, organizations can, and almost always do, institute specific improvements at any time they choose, even before they are prepared to advance to the level at which the specific practice is optimized. Organizations should understand, however, that the effectiveness, stability, and value of these improvements are at greater risk because the foundation for their successful institutionalization has not been fully established.

At the same time, it must be recognized that process improvement efforts should focus on the needs of the organization in the context of its business environment and that higher-level practices may address the current needs of the organization. Therefore, we focus on both organizational needs and practices at the next maturity level when conducting assessments and planning process improvement initiatives.

The Levels of the CompassBA/PM™ Organizational Maturity Model

The stages of the CompassBA/PM™ OMM are defined below.

Level 1: Informal

At maturity level 1, processes are often chaotic. Business analysis, project management, and systems engineering practices are ad hoc and informal. Practices are performed inconsistently in pockets across the organization.

At maturity level 1, the organization usually does not provide a stable environment. Success in the organization depends on the competence and heroics of the people in the organization and not on the use of proven processes. In spite of this ad hoc, chaotic environment, maturity level 1 organizations often produce products and services that work; however, these organizations frequently exceed the budget and schedule of their projects, and sometimes fail to deliver anything of value to the customer. Maturity level 1 organizations have a tendency to overcommit, to abandon processes in the time of crisis, and to not be able to repeat their past successes.[3]

Level 2: Documented

Level 2 practices include those that bring about basic management control of projects.

Description

The projects of the organization have ensured that requirements are managed and that processes are planned, performed, measured, and controlled. Business analysis, project management, and systems engineering practices for level 2 are institutionalized across the organization. Institutionalization involves implementing a corporate culture that supports the methods, practices, and procedures of the business so that they endure after those who originally defined them have left the organization. When these practices are in place, projects are performed and managed according to their documented plans.

At maturity level 2, requirements, processes, work products, and services are managed. The status of the work products and the delivery of services are visible to management at defined points (e.g., at major milestones and control gate reviews). Commitments are established among stakeholders and are revised as needed. Work products are reviewed with stakeholders, and changes to the work products are controlled.[4]

Mastery

Level 2 maturity includes mastery of the knowledge and skills and institutionalization of the following practices:

+ IIBA *BABOK™ Guide* practices: requirements planning and management, including the ability to manage all requirements received or generated by the project, both technical and nontechnical

+ PMI *PMBOK® Guide* knowledge areas: integration, scope, time, cost, and procurement management

+ SEI CMMI® process areas: requirements management, project planning, project monitoring and control, supplier agreement management, performance measurement and analysis, and configuration management. (Note: SEI places process and product quality assurance (QA) at level 2, whereas this model places QA at level 3 based on the premise that basic control is needed before QA techniques can be applied.)

Project Management Criteria

Basic project management criteria that project teams meet to achieve level 2 include (1) defining the scope of work in a charter or statement of work (SOW) or other scope definition document and decomposing the scope of work in a work breakdown structure (WBS); (2) planning and scheduling the work embodied in the WBS into a project schedule with interdependencies linked to form a network diagram; (3) assigning resources and estimating the work effort based on work interruption factors, skill factors, and the part-time effect (accounting for when team members are working on multiple activities simultaneously, adding time to the base estimates for them to switch between activities); (4) budgeting work packages to cost accounts relating to functional areas; (5) maintaining a performance baseline; (6) monitoring performance against the baseline and implementing corrective actions to maintain the baseline; (7) managing changes to the baseline and establishing a new baseline when increase in scope is approved or performance indicates that a new baseline is required; (8) managing configurations of work products as they are developed and revised; and (9) managing all subcontractor agreements.

Business Analysis Criteria

Basic business analysis criteria that project teams meet to achieve level 2 include (1) planning all requirement activities and artifacts to be produced, (2) archiving and storing requirements artifacts, and (3) managing changes to requirements throughout the product development life cycle.

Organizational Criteria

In addition, basic organizational criteria that must be met to achieve level 2 maturity include (1) project monitoring and control and (2) executive oversight of project performance (typically at key control gate reviews).

Level 3: Integrated

Advanced business analysis and project management practices enable the organization to successfully manage significant, high-risk, complex projects. At maturity level 3, an organization has achieved all the goals of the process areas assigned to maturity levels 2 and 3.

Description

At maturity level 3, processes are well defined and well understood, and they are documented in organizational standards, procedures, tools, and methods. Project teams establish their processes by tailoring the set of organizational standards according to tailoring guidelines. The organization establishes process objectives based on organizational standard processes and ensures that those objectives are appropriately addressed.

A critical distinction between maturity level 2 and maturity level 3 is the scope of standards, process descriptions, and procedures, and the level of QA needed to enforce compliance to standards. At maturity level 2, the standards, process descriptions, and procedures may be quite different in each specific instance of the process (for example, on a particular project). At maturity level 3, the standards, process descriptions, and procedures for a project are tailored from the set of organizational standards to suit a particular project or organizational unit. At maturity level 3, processes are defined more specifically and managed more proactively using an understanding of the interrelationships of the process activities and detailed measures of the process, its work products, and its services. The set of organizational standards includes the processes addressed at maturity levels 2 and 3.[5]

Mastery

Level 3 maturity includes mastery of the knowledge and skills and institutionalization of the following practices:

* IIBA *BABOK*™ *Guide* practices: producing and analyzing customer and product requirements, including defined techniques for requirements elicitation, requirements analysis and documentation, requirements communication, and requirements implementation

* PMI *PMBOK*® *Guide* knowledge areas: risk, human resource, quality, and communications management, including earned value management (EVM), performance management, stakeholder management, and the ability to traverse the organizational culture, power, politics, and cross-dependencies

* SEI CMMI® process areas: requirements development, technical solution, product integration, verification, validation, organizational process focus, organizational process definition, organizational training, integrated project management, risk management, integrated teaming, integrated supplier management, decision analysis and resolution, and organizational environment for integration

Project Management Criteria

Project management criteria that project teams meet to achieve level 3 include (1) advanced risk management, including quantitative risk assessment and risk response planning; (2) quality management, including applying effective quality control and quality assurance practices; (3) advanced communication techniques, including measuring performance using EVM techniques; (4) managing the environment embodied in cultural nuances, power, politics, cross-dependencies, and differing and sometimes conflicting stakeholder expectations; and (5) human resource management, involving building and maintaining high-performing core teams composed of the project manager, the business analyst, and business representative(s) and the systems engineer, the technical architect, and the lead developer.

Business Analysis Criteria

Business analysis criteria that project teams meet to achieve level 3 involve the tasks that encompass all the activities involved in gathering, evaluating, and documenting requirements, including (1) scope and business domain definition, (2) requirements elicitation, (3) requirements analysis, (4) requirements specification, (5) requirements documentation, (6) requirements validation, (7) requirements verification, and (8) collaboration with the system engineer and the design and development team to determine the optimum technical solution and achieve product integration.

Organizational Criteria

In addition, more advanced organizational criteria that must be met to achieve level 3 maturity include (1) organizational process quality focus, including the formation of a quality assurance and/or test group; (2) organizational process definition; (3) organizational training; (4) integrated project management; (5) integrated teaming; (6) integrated supplier management; (7) integrated decision analysis and resolution; (8) documented organizational policies and standards; and (9) organizational environment for total project, program, and portfolio integration.

Level 4: Strategic

At maturity level 4, business analysis and project management have been elevated to a strategic management practice. Cultural and organizational behaviors, structures, and processes are in place to ensure that projects are strategically aligned. At this level, an organization has achieved all the specific goals of the process areas assigned to maturity levels 2, 3, and 4.

Description

At maturity level 4, subprocesses that significantly contribute to overall process performance are selected. These selected subprocesses are controlled using statistical and other quantitative techniques.

Quantitative objectives for quality and process performance are established and used as criteria in managing processes. They are based on the needs of the customer, end users, organization, and process implementers. Quality and process performance are understood in statistical terms and are managed throughout the life of the project. Quality and process performance measures are incorporated into the organizational measurement repository to support fact-based decision making in the future. A critical distinction between maturity level 3 and maturity level 4 is the predictability of performance.[6]

Mastery

Level 4 maturity includes mastery of the knowledge and skills and institutionalization of the following practices:

- IIBA *BABOK™ Guide* practices: enterprise analysis activities, including strategic planning, strategic goal-setting, corporate scorecard development and implementation, and project selection and management based on value

+ PMI areas of focus: program and portfolio management

+ SEI CMMI® process areas: organizational process performance, quantitative quality management, and quantitative project performance measurement

Project Management Criteria

Elements of organizations practicing level 4 project management include the following: (1) robust strategic plans that are converted to strategic goals and measured through a corporate scorecard exist; (2) a strategic approach to portfolio management exists so that projects are strategically aligned and managed throughout the project life cycle; (3) projects report against corporate scorecard metrics; (4) organizational resource management is practiced, allocating resources to the highest-priority projects first; and (5) executive oversight is evidenced by project sponsor committees and periodic control gate reviews that are conducted at major project milestones to reassess the project cost, schedule, scope, quality, risk, and expected benefits to the organization, followed by go/no go decisions to continue to invest in the project.

Business Analysis Criteria

Elements of organizations practicing level 4 business analysis include robust pre-project business opportunity analyses to provide the governance group with the information needed to make the best project investment decisions. These analyses include (1) business architecture development; (2) feasibility, benchmark, and competitive analysis studies; (3) business opportunity identification and alternative solution analysis; (4) new opportunity scoping and proposed project definition; (5) business case development; and (6) initial risk assessment. In addition, the actual business value achieved by the project results are tracked, analyzed, and reported to the project portfolio governance group to determine whether the project investment was sound and the project execution was optimized.

Organizational Criteria

Organizational criteria that must be met to achieve level 4 maturity include (1) an enterprise business analysis/project management center of excellence and departmental centers (often called project management offices), both of which support portfolio investment decisions and project team execution, exist; (2) a robust strategic planning committee that reviews and refines strategies as business needs change exists; (3) a robust corporate scorecard system is in place; (4) resources are allocated to the higher-priority projects first; and (5) executive project sponsor committees exist, and a fully engaged project governance group exists to constantly monitor projects for reassessment and reprioritization.

Level 5: Optimized

Business analysis, project management, and systems engineering in a level 5 organization are distinguished by vibrant, continuous process improvement. The organization emphasizes continuous improvement to its project-related practices. This level requires an organization to measure effectiveness and continually implement improvements to processes, tools, and techniques. The goal is to put in place improvements that will provide timely decision making, reduce project costs, and improve project performance. At maturity level 5, an organization has achieved all the specific goals of the process areas assigned to maturity levels 2, 3, 4, and 5.

Description

At maturity level 5, processes are continually improved on the basis of a quantitative understanding of the common causes of variation inherent in processes. Maturity level 5 focuses on continually improving process performance through incremental and innovative technological improvements. Quantitative process-improvement objectives for the organization are established, continually revised to reflect changing business objectives, and used as criteria in managing process improvement. The effects of deployed process improvements are measured and evaluated against the quantitative process-improvement objectives. Both the defined processes and the set of organizational standards are targets of measurable improvement activities.

Optimizing processes that are agile and innovative depends on the participation of an empowered workforce aligned with the business values and objectives of the organization. The organizational ability to rapidly respond to changes and opportunities is enhanced by finding ways to accelerate and share learning. Improvement of the processes is inherently part of everybody's role, resulting in a cycle of continual improvement.[7]

Mastery

Level 5 maturity includes mastery of the knowledge and skills and institutionalization of the following practices:

+ IIBA *BABOK*™ *Guide* practices: measuring the actual business value that resulted from project results, conducting root-cause analysis of unintended consequences (e.g., why projected benefits were not achieved), and incorporating lessons learned into the portfolio selection, prioritization, and management processes.

+ PMI areas of focus: methods for evaluating best practices and capabilities, and capability improvement aggregating to best practices[8]

+ SEI CMMI® process areas: organizational innovation and deployment, and causal analysis and resolution

Project Management Criteria

Elements of organizations practicing level 5 project management include (1) continuous evaluation of project management organizational maturity, (2) project management improvement initiatives, (3) implementation of project management improvements, (4) evaluation of the effectiveness of changes, and (5) project manager knowledge and skill assessments, followed by development programs linked to strategic goals.

Business Analysis Criteria

Elements of organizations practicing level 5 business analysis include (1) continuous evaluation of business analysis organizational maturity, (2) continuous business analysis improvement initiatives, (3) implementation of business analysis improvements, (4) evaluation of the effectiveness of changes, and (5) individual business analyst knowledge and skill assessments, followed by development programs linked to strategic goals.

Organizational Criteria

Organizational criteria that must be met to achieve level 5 maturity include (1) maturity assessments conducted by the enterprise business analysis/project management center of excellence and departmental centers (often called project management offices), both of which support portfolio investment decisions and project team execution; (2) continuous improvements to strategic planning process and to strategic goal-setting process; (3) continuous improvements to project reporting process against corporate scorecard metrics; (4) continuous improvements to organization-wide portfolio and resource management, including project selection and prioritization and ongoing review and management of the portfolio; (5) continuous improvements to executive oversight process; and (6) periodic and consistent project audits, for both healthy and troubled projects, to continuously improve project processes.

Endnotes

1. Parviz F. Rad and Ginger Levin. *The Advanced Project Management Office*, 2002. Boca Raton, FL: CRC Press, LLC.

2. Carnegie Mellon Software Engineering Institute. *Capability Maturity Model® Integration (CMMI®)*, Version 1.1. CMMI® for Systems Engineering, Software Engineering, Integrated Product and Process Development, and Supplier Sourcing (CMMI-SE/SW/IPPD/SS, V1.1). Staged Representation. CMU/SEI-2002-TR-012, ESC-TR-2002-012, March 2002. Online at http://www.sei.cmu.edu/cmmi/models/ss-staged-v1.1.doc#_ Toc2041596 (accessed November 1, 2005).

3. ibid.

4. ibid.

5. ibid.

6. ibid.

7. ibid.

8. Project Management Institute. *Organizational Project Management Maturity Model (OPM3) Knowledge Foundation*, 2003. Newtown Square, PA: Project Management Institute.

Epilogue

So there you have it—a broad view of the emerging profession of business analysis. By now you have come to realize that the business analyst's role is both strategic and tactical, and that it is rapidly coming into its own. The business analyst, as a key member of the project leadership team, provides the strong business focus and clear, usable requirements that have been missing from most projects with a significant IT component.

Because organizations depend on project success for their very survival, business analysts must hone their ability to be proactive, equip themselves with capabilities to anticipate project challenges, and adapt their approach as they learn more about the project. Most of all, they must learn how to form a strong partnership with other project leaders (the project manager, lead architects and developers, and business visionaries) and build high-performing teams.

As you begin to develop your business analyst knowledge and skills, may I suggest that you use other volumes in the Business Analysis Essential Library series as important resources to help you perform well in specific situations:

+ If you have been asked to participate in an effort to prepare a business case for a new project:

  □ *The Business Analyst as Strategist: Translating Business Strategies into Valuable Solutions* provides information about the business analysis activities that should be performed to ensure your organization is investing in the most profitable projects. Do remember that the activities that are recommended are for large-scale organizational change efforts requiring significant investments. For lower risk, lower cost projects, not all of the activities will likely be needed. However, a business case is needed for all projects, with the exception of minor maintenance and enhancement tasks.

* If you have been assigned as a business analyst to a newly approved project:

  □ Refer to *Unearthing Business Requirements: Elicitation Tools and Techniques* for an overview of how to plan requirements activities and embark upon the requirements elicitation efforts.

  □ Refer to *The Art and Power of Facilitation: Running Powerful Meetings* for effective tools and techniques to use when planning elicitation workshops, interviews, and focus group sessions.

  □ Refer to *Getting It Right: Business Requirement Analysis Tools and Techniques* for valuable tools and techniques to analyze, specify, and validate the requirements.

* If you are interested in elevating your role and becoming an essential business and/or technology consultant for your organization:

  □ Refer to *From Analyst to Leader: Elevating the Role of the Business Analyst* for guidance about building your leadership skills, developing high-performing teams, leading complex projects, and implementing a business analysis center of excellence in your organization.

Index

R

RAM. *See* responsibility assignment matrix
requirement, definition, 51
requirements analysis
  allocating, 60
  assessing risk and constraints, 59
  business analyst, 63
  clarifying and restating, 59
  context diagramming, 58
  creating test cases, 59
  decomposing, 59
  defining terms, 59
  deriving, 59
  developing business scenarios, 60
  modeling, 59
  overview, 57–58
  prioritizing, 59
  prototyping, 59
  studying, 58
  trading off, 59
requirements categories
  functional *versus* nonfunctional, 62–63
  importance of, 61–62
requirements documentation
  business analyst, 70
  characteristics of, 66–67
requirements elicitation
  business analyst, 55–56
  document review, 54
  elicitation workshops, 53–54
  feedback loops, 55
  gathering, 53
  interviews, 54
  note-taking, 55
  observation, 55
  overview, 51–52

prior to elicitation, 52–53
  surveys, 54
requirements engineering
  agile development, 80–83
  change, 79–80
  importance of, 8–10
  iteration, 83–84
  project complexity model, 85–86
  scalability, 84–85
requirements generation, 30
requirements management
  allocating, 69
  business analyst, 70
  importance of, 68–69
  managing changes, 69
  tracing, 69
  validating and verifying, 69–70
requirements specification
  acceptance criteria, 61
  author, 61
  business analyst, 63
  complexity indicator, 61
  overview, 60
  ownership, 61
  performance, 61
  priority, 61
  source, 61
  stability indicator, 61
  status, 61
  unique identifiers, 60–61
  urgency, 61
requirements validation
  business analyst, 70
  characteristics of, 67–68
responsibility assignment
  matrix (RAM), 23
role definition, 17